Travel Guide

COSTA DEL SOL

D1809836

SUE BRYANT

NEW HOLLAND

NEW HOLLAND

This edition first published in 2000
by New Holland Publishers (UK) Ltd
London • Cape Town • Sydney • Auckland
First published in 1996
10 9 8 7 6 5 4

24 Nutford Place
London W1H 6DQ
United Kingdom

80 McKenzie Street
Cape Town 8001
South Africa

14 Aquatic Drive
Frenchs Forest, NSW 2086
Australia

218 Lake Road
Northcote, Auckland
New Zealand

Copyright © 2000 in text: Sue Bryant
Copyright © 2000 in maps: Globetrotter
Travel Maps
Copyright © 2000 in photographs:
Individual photographers as credited (right).
Copyright © 2000 New Holland Publishers (UK) Ltd

ISBN 1 85974 069 3

Commisioning Editor: Tim Jollands
Manager Globetrotter Maps: John Loubser
Editors: Thea Grobbelaar, Sara Harper,
Nune Jordaan
Design and DTP: Gillian Black
Cartographer: Éloïse Moss
Compiler/Verifier: Elaine Fick
Reproduction by Hirt & Carter (Pty) Ltd, Cape Town
Printed and bound in Hong Kong by Sing Cheong
Printing Co. Ltd.

Although every effort has been made to ensure
accuracy of facts, and telephone and fax numbers in this book, the publishers will not be held
responsible for changes that occur at the time of
going to press.

Acknowledgements:
The author would like to thank Carlos de Garriz and
José Antonio Secilla of CYRASA; the Costa del Sol
Tourist Promotion Board; Spanish Tourist Board;
Viva Air; Hotel Alay, Benalmádena; the Marbella
Club; Hotel Alcora, Sevilla; and Autos Lara,
Torremolinos.

Photographic Credits:
Stephen Andrews (Travel Ink), page 63; **Adrian
Baker** (PhotoBank), page 81; **Jeanetta Baker**
(PhotoBank), page 111; **Peter Baker** (PhotoBank),
front cover, pages 32, 52, 75, 96, 98; **Tony Baker**
(PhotoBank), page 92; **Rodney Badkin** (Travel Ink),
pages 28, 30; **Elly Beintema** (RHPL), page 102 (left
and right); **Nigel Blythe** (RHPL), page 113; **C.
Bowman** (RHPL), page 65; **The Bridgeman Art
Library** (Museo de Bellas Artes, Seville), page 37;
Sue Bryant, pages 8, 22, 29, 39, 40, 118, 119; **Martyn
F. Chillmaid** (RHPL), page 99; **Fin Costello** (RHPL),
page 18; **Rob Cousins** (RHPL), pages 76, 114, 116;
F. P. G. International (RHPL), page 16; **Robert
Francis** (RHPL), pages 77, 100; **Robert Frerck**
(RHPL), pages 6, 10, 12, 21, 35, 56, 69; **Gail Goodger**
(The Hutchison Library), page 62; **Juliet Highet**
(Life File), page 101 (left and right); **Roger G.
Howard**, page 48; **Brenda Kean** (Travel Ink), page 25;
The Kobal Collection, page 103; **Emma Lee** (Life
File), pages 41, 54, 115; **J. Lightfoot** (RHPL), page 26;
Duncan Maxwell (RHPL), pages 38, 95, 107; **John
Mills** (RHPL), page 72; **PhotoBank**, pages 17, 44;
Picture Bank Photo Library, page 23, 68; **Brian
Richards**, page 15, 67; **G. R. Richardson** (RHPL),
page 85; **Robert Harding Picture Library**, pages 4, 7,
9, 20, 47, 49, 50, 53, 55, 57, 60, 78, 80, 90, 97; **Sheila
Terry** (RHPL), pages 14, 79, 82, 83; **Adina Tovy**
(RHPL), page 106; **Peter Wilson**, title page, pages 19,
31, 112, 117; **Nik Wheeler** (RHPL), page 88; **T. D.
Winter** (RHPL), page 13, 27; **Adam Woolfitt**
(RHPL), page 11; **Zefa**, page 24.

Cover: *Nerja's beach as seen from Balcón de Europa.*
Title Page: *Traditional flamenco dancing.*

CONTENTS

1
Introducing the Costa del Sol

Spain's 'sunshine coast' forms the southern fringe of the region of **Andalucía**, bordered to the west by the **Rock of Gibraltar** and to the east by the mountains of **Almería**. With about 320 days of blue sky annually and an endless string of sandy beaches, it's not surprising that over two million tourists a year flock to the area, making it one of Europe's most successful holiday destinations.

Yet despite the march of development that has peppered the narrow coastal strip with high-rise hotels and sprawling timeshare developments, the Costa del Sol manages to encapsulate all that is Spanish: scented orange groves and rolling fields of silver olive trees; the passion of the bullfight and the rhythm of flamenco; tiny bars in winding backstreets where locals sip chilled **Jerez** wines and laughter mingles with the aroma of fried garlic.

It is this contrast that makes the region so appealing. Within minutes of the coast is a part of Spain that most of the sun, sea and sangria-loving tourists never discover. Wander through the lovely old town of **Málaga**, birthplace of Picasso; hike the mountain trails looking out across the Mediterranean to **Africa**; follow the 'route of the bulls' around **Sevilla** or try freshly grilled sardines on the beach at **Torremolinos**.

Life on the Costa del Sol is very relaxed and the local people welcome both ends of the tourist spectrum, from the yacht-dwellers of **Puerto Banús** to the families attracted by the gently shelving beaches and easy lifestyle. This cosmopolitan atmosphere is the magnet that brings people back again and again.

TOP ATTRACTIONS

*** Granada: the last of the great Moorish cities, packed with architectural interest.
*** The Pueblos Blancos: dazzling white villages, perched high in the mountains behind the coast.
*** Las Alpujarras: the high villages of the Sierra Nevada.
** Ronda: hilltop town clinging to the sides of a deep gorge and regarded as the birthplace of bullfighting.
* Marbella: playground of the wealthy.

Opposite: *Millionaires' yachts line the marina at Puerto Banús.*

Right: *Shady pine trees scent the air along the coast and inland.*
Opposite: *Vast cultivated fields and hillsides dotted with olives form typical scenery around Córdoba.*

THE LAND

The region of Andalucía is the largest and most geographically diverse in Spain, its coastal terrain ranging from high, snow-capped mountains to long, sandy beaches and from swampy marshland to rock-strewn desert. Further inland, mountains give way to rolling hills and cultivated plains, brilliant yellow with sunflowers in spring. Several 'costas' make up its coastline, from the relatively unknown **Costa de la Luz** in the west to the **Costa de Almería** in the far east. The longest and busiest stretch, the **Costa del Sol**, is between the two, extending from the tiny British colony of **Gibraltar** to just east of **Málaga**. The eastern stretch of the Costa del Sol, which forms the coastline of mountainous **Granada** province, is subtitled the **Costa Tropical** because of its humid microclimate.

Málaga province itself covers approximately 7254km² (2800 sq miles) and at just north of 36° latitude, is one of Europe's most southerly areas. The provincial capital, Málaga is further south than the Greek capital of **Athens** and the North African cities of **Algiers** and **Tunis**.

Mountains and Rivers

The Costa del Sol itself is a narrow, fertile strip of coast-line, flanked by steep mountains on one side and shelving gently into the Mediterranean on the other. While the mountains are bleached out and scrub-covered by the end of the hot summers, the carefully tended coast is a riot of colour. One emerald golf course after another is interspersed with scarlet, purple and orange tropical flowers and luxuriant gardens of banana palms, orange trees and fragrant jasmine bushes scent the air.

Immediately behind the coastal mountains is the broad valley of the **Guadalquivir River**, which meanders from its source in the **Cazorla Mountains** of Jaén across its floodplain through the cities of Sevilla and Córdoba (402km; 250 miles) to the sea. The Guadalquivir feeds several smaller rivers which have created dramatic rock formations as they cut through the limestone rock. One of the most striking examples is the gorge of **El Chorro**, a rugged canyon just 50km (31 miles) to the north of Málaga not far from **El Torcal**, a mountainous area of bizarre limestone formations.

Beyond Marbella, the steep **Sierra Bermeja** mountain range, the beginning of the dramatic **Serranía de Ronda**, rises sharply from the coastal plain to form one of the region's most beautiful areas of deep gorges, rare pine forests and rushing torrents, with tiny white villages scattered like icing sugar over the hilltops. Typical limestone scenery is prevalent in this region, with several caves containing stalactites and stalagmites, open to the public.

Tejeda forms the foothills of the **Sierra Nevada**, Spain's highest mountain range, rising up to 3300m (10,827ft) and covered by snow for most of the year. But this is a region of tremendous geographical contrast and further east still is yet another world, where the Sierra Nevada gives way to the mountain desert scenery of **Almería** province, and setting for many a Hollywood blockbuster.

MAGIC ANDALUCIA

Certain phenomena in Andalucía were believed to have magical powers in ancient superstition. The wind-eroded rocks of **El Torcal**, the gorge of **El Chorro** and the prehistoric **dolmens** around Antequera were thought to be the work of giants that once inhabited the area and the drawings of strange animals on the wall of **La Pileta** caves near Ronda were considered sacred.

Animals were symbolic too – a **bull** signified creative power, while a **horse** meant life after death. **Olives** symbolized peace, fertility and purification, while a **boar** meant the devil, the destroyer of fields and vineyards.

Seas and Shores

The western side of the Costa del Sol ends at the British colony of **Gibraltar**, clustered around the base of a sheer chunk of uplifted limestone jutting out into the **Mediterranean**. The northern tip of **Africa**, usually purple in the heat haze, is a mere 8km (5 miles) across the narrow Strait of Gibraltar. **Málaga**, the capital of the eponymous province, is at the geographical centre of the coast and the areas immediately to the east and west are the most densely populated.

East of **Málaga**, the coast is less populated and agriculture, not tourism, is the principal land use, avocado and sugar plantations and peach orchards bordering mostly stony bays. Around **Nerja**, another Sierra (which means 'mountains'), **Tejeda**, falls dramatically into the sea, reducing the long stretches of beach to small coves. Just inland are the dramatic limestone caves of Nerja, one of which contains the world's largest stalactite. Beaches along the Costa del Sol vary from rather disappointing strips of grey grit around Málaga to long sweeps of sand further west. Of the big resorts, **Torremolinos** is a sun-worshipper's dream; two huge half-moons of sand lined with bars, restaurants and brightly coloured sun umbrellas. East of Málaga the coast is steep and rocky so the best swimming and snorkelling is from small coves. For such a densely populated region, the sea is surprisingly clean, with several beaches awarded a blue flag by the EU for their high environmental standards.

Climate

Protected by the coastal mountain ranges from the climatic extremes of inland Andalucía, the Costa del Sol basks in about 320 days of **sunshine** a year, enjoying long, hot summers and mild winters. Humidity is low and summer evenings are balmy.

If it's going to **rain**, it does so in winter – from **December** to **March** – and four or five consecutive days of grey skies are not unusual. But even then, temperatures rarely fall below 10–11ºC (50–52ºF), which is warm enough for shirtsleeves. What visitors should be aware of is the dramatic temperature changes at higher altitudes: a pleasant day on the coast may be several degrees more chilly just half an hour into the mountains.

Away from the coast, the Andalucían summers are less forgiving, with the cities of Jerez de la Frontera and Sevilla often sweltering on the sun-baked inland plains in over 40°C (104°F). The best time for touring, therefore, is **spring**, when the hills are carpeted with wild flowers, the almond trees are in blossom and the pavement cafés are beginning to fill up.

The Sierra Nevada, the craggy mountain range surrounding the city of Granada, offers yet another climatic extreme, with heavy **snowfall** in winter making it Spain's most popular ski area. Just 40km (25 miles) from the coast, the road climbs to about 3300m (10,827ft) and the temperature plummets to below zero. The mountains have snowy caps for most of the year, although the summer months are perfect for hiking and mountain biking.

Flora and Fauna

The vegetation of the Costa del Sol is typical of the southern Mediterranean, with hillsides of gnarled, silvery **olive** trees and cool forests of **pine**, **cork** and **oak**. **Grapes** are grown around Jerez and Málaga, and **wheat** and **sunflowers** are farmed on the plains of the Guadalquivir River. **Orange** and **lemon trees** grow in orchards and in gardens and village squares.

East of Málaga the coastal plain is a sea of **peach** and **cherry** orchards and **tomato** greenhouses. Much fruit is farmed and **mango** and **custard apple** are also grown here. Around Motril in Granada province are Europe's only **sugar cane** plantations.

Above: *In spring, almond blossom scents the air and covers the hillsides.*
Opposite: *Rocky cliffs and sheltered bays east of Málaga contrast with the long, sandy beaches of the west.*

COMPARATIVE CLIMATE CHART	MALAGA				GRANADA				SEVILLA			
	WIN	SPR	SUM	AUT	WIN	SPR	SUM	AUT	WIN	SPR	SUM	AUT
	JAN	APR	JULY	OCT	JAN	APR	JULY	OCT	JAN	APR	JULY	OCT
MAX TEMP. °C	17	21	32	23	12	20	34	23	15	24	36	26
MIN TEMP. °C	8	13	21	16	2	7	17	10	6	11	20	14
MAX TEMP. °F	63	70	70	73	54	68	93	73	59	75	97	79
MIN TEMP. °F	46	55	70	61	36	45	63	50	43	52	68	57
HOURS OF SUN	6	10	10	6	5	10	10	6	6	10	11	6
RAINFALL in	6	4.3	1	6	4	1.8	0.3	4	4	1.8	0.3	2.3
RAINFALL mm	150	108	25	150	100	46	8	67	100	46	8	58

Inland, vast tracts of the coastal mountains have been designated national park and a brief journey may reward the visitor with glimpses of **mountain hare**, **deer**, **wild partridge** and the **Spanish ibex** (wild Iberian mountain goat). **Golden eagles** and **griffon vultures** wheel in the sky over the high mountain passes of the Serranía de Ronda and **otters** inhabit the trout streams, much to the displeasure of local farmers. Much of the area around Ronda is highly protected, as its unique microclimate is the only place in the world where the **pinsapo fir**, *Abeis pinsapo*, grows. The trees are believed to have been pushed south by the ice sheets in the ice age and remained, stranded, when the ice retreated. There are some surprises, too: about 20km (12 miles) northwest of Antequera is the **Laguna de Fuente de Piedra**: the largest natural lake in Andalucía and Europe's only inland breeding ground for the **greater flamingo**.

In the Guadalquivir Valley, farming of **cattle** and **horses** plays an important role. But this is five-star farming, where Spain's most expensive and aggressive **bulls** are bred and trained for the bullring. Here, too, the exquisite Andalucían **horses** are raised on wealthy ranches, or *fincas*, either for dressage or for their role in the *corrida*.

HISTORY IN BRIEF

The strategic position of the southern coast of Spain and its proximity to North Africa means its history is quite different to that of the rest of Spain. Almost 800 years (711–1492) as a **Moorish** (collective name for numerous waves of Arab, Syrian and Berber settlers from North Africa) empire has given **Andalucía** a unique artistic and cultural heritage and the influence of the **Moors** is apparent in architecture everywhere, from the smallest village to the most spectacular monument.

Pre-Roman Times

The first known inhabitants of the area lived in caves around what is now Málaga province, leaving wall paintings dating from 25,000BC at **Nerja**, east of Málaga and at **La Pileta**, near Ronda, of the animals they hunted. Early architecture dating from 2500BC is evident at **Antequera**, an hour's drive north of Málaga, where primitive Iberian tribes built the dolmens: cave tombs guarded by massive stones.

Around 1100BC, sophisticated Phoenicians arrived from what is now Lebanon, founding settlements at Cádiz and Málaga and introducing the concept of currency. Greek traders established colonies around 650BC, enjoying a brief period of wealth thanks to Andalucía's rich mineral deposits. Olives and grapes, two important crops today, were introduced at this time.

The Greeks were soon ousted by the Carthaginians, people from Carthage (near present-day Tunis) in North Africa, who

Opposite: *Ronda's dazzling whiteness is offset by fields of scarlet poppies in spring.*
Left: *The burial chambers around Antequera are in a remarkable state of preservation for their age – 4500 years old.*

MOORISH ARCHITECTURE

While the Moors were deeply religious, they did tend to live life according to an old Arab proverb that the 'nights are for sleeping and the days for resting' and their architecture reflects both characteristics. Rooms in palaces like the **Alhambra** are bare because the Moors had little furniture. Visitors would sit on cushions and stone floors would be covered with rugs and *kelims*. Because much time was spent reclining and gazing upwards, ceilings are always ornate.

As the Koran expressly forbids the representation of people and animals in art, artistic expression was channelled into brilliantly coloured mosaic patterns and elaborate inscriptions, both from the Koran and from the poets of the time. The strange, stalactite formations on ceilings in the Alhambra represent the cave in which the prophet **Mohammed** was supposed to have written the Koran, while the **suns**, **moons** and stars on the ceilings represent heaven.

moved in and occupied most of Andalucía, using the region's mineral wealth to finance a huge military presence. Under the general Hannibal, they prepared to attack Rome but were defeated in the Second Punic War in 214BC.

Romans, Vandals and Visigoths

The Romans, welcomed by the Andalucían people in 210BC after years of oppression, began to build on an unprecedented scale, remnants of which can be seen in the aqueduct of Nerja, the Roman theatre in Málaga and even the N340 coastal highway, an early version of which connected Cádiz with Rome. The region was named **Baetica** with Córdoba as its capital and 400 years of prosperity followed during which time the Latin language, Roman law and Christianity became firmly established. The people enjoyed the fruits of a thriving industry in wine, olive oil, wool and grain.

Eventually, however, the Roman Empire crumbled and Baetica was invaded by barbarian tribes from northern Europe. First to arrive in AD409 were the Vandals, who named the area **Vandalusía**, and shortly afterwards the Visigoths, a Germanic race of Aryan Christians ostensibly allied with Rome, who promptly claimed Roman lands for themselves and ruled for 300 years.

Right: *Córdoba's magnificent Puente Romano is part of the city's Roman heritage.*
Opposite: *Rich colour and intricate arches are typical features of Moorish architecture.*

Moorish Influence

The Moors, assorted Berber and Arab North African tribes united by their Muslim faith, saw an opportunity to move into the still-wealthy Vandalusía. In AD711, under the leadership of Tariq, then governor of Tangier, a vast Berber army crossed the Strait of Gibraltar and forced the Visigoths north into the mountains after the **Battle of Guadalete**, close to Jerez. Some 800 years of Moorish rule followed in the newly named Kingdom of **al-Andalus**.

The tolerant attitude of the **Moors** meant that Jews, Christians and Muslims lived in harmony and a period of great wealth and cultural development began, during which time the architecture, philosophy and learning developed quickly. Oranges and peaches were cultivated and ceramics, leather and silverware were crafted. Rather than destroying what had gone before them, the Moors used Roman buildings as a basis for further development, adding their own style to form the astonishingly beautiful monuments that can be seen today in **Córdoba**, **Granada** and **Sevilla**.

Everything began to slowly fall apart around the 11th century. The ruler Abd-ar-Rahman III had established himself in 928 as Caliph of Córdoba but his weaker successors let the caliphate disintegrate until 1031, when it split up into a series of *taifas*: small kingdoms which were constantly squabbling. The **Christian** armies of northern Spain moved in and captured the *taifa* of Toledo. The Moors had to call for reinforcements, which brought a wave of Islamic fanaticism as the puritanical **Almoravids** from North Africa came into power in 1086. After 60 terrifying years, a more tolerant sect, the **Almohads** drove them out and set about rebuilding al-Andalus, only to be defeated themselves by the Christians at the **Battle of Las Navas de Tolosa** in 1212, which was the beginning of the end for Moorish Spain.

Right: *Every tile tells a story in Sevilla's Plaza de España.*
Opposite: *Málaga's English Cemetery was founded by British Consul-General William Mark in 1830.*

The Reconquest and the Catholic Kings

Over the next 200 years, Moorish *taifas* of al-Andalus were captured one by one by the Christian forces. The last enclave, Granada, was conquered in 1492, the same year that **Columbus** landed in the West Indies. The New World had been discovered and Spain entered a new era under the dynastic partnership of **Ferdinand of Aragón** and **Isabella of Castile**, *Los Reyes Católicos*, or Catholic kings, as they were dubbed by the Pope.

Despite promises of religious freedom after the capture of Granada, Ferdinand and Isabella proceeded to persecute **Jews** and **Muslims**, eventually expelling anybody who would not freely convert to Christianity and causing those who had converted to flee in terror. Moorish land and possessions were divided among wealthy Christians, creating a system of land ownership which has dogged Andalucía ever since. While the rest of Spain basked in the glory of its overseas conquests and their subsequent wealth, Andalucía deteriorated into a poverty-stricken backwater, subject to frequent raids by **Barbary pirates**. People fled inland to the Sierras, neglecting the coast which once again became an uncultivated desert. In 1516 **Carlos I**, a member of the Hapsburg dynasty, came to the throne and was elected **Charles V**, Emperor of the Holy Roman Empire. During his reign he neglected Spain in favour of Rome and the country's wealth was further drained.

GOYA

Francisco José de Goya y Lucientes (1746–1828), regarded as one of the three greats of his time alongside El Greco and Velázquez, was born near **Zaragoza**. From the age of 14, he studied as an apprentice painter and in 1786 was court painter to Carlos III, popular because of his candid cartoons of everyday life. Paintings of bullfighting scenes from his days in Ronda with the great bullfighter Pedro Romero are re-enacted every year at Ronda's *goyesca* festival, with matadors in traditional dress.

Some of Goya's later, important works include *The Disasters of War* series from 1810, based on the atrocities of the Napoleonic occupation of Spain, and two paintings: *Second and Third of May, 1808* which depict massacres of unarmed Spaniards by French soldiers. Goya died in **Bordeaux**, France, in 1824.

A new inquisition under Felipe II and his successor, Felipe III, led to a final purging of Muslims and Jews, depriving the country of much skilled labour. The **Spanish Armada** was sunk in 1588 as Felipe II attempted to invade England and expensive forays into the New World forced Spain further into debt.

Bourbons

For the next two centuries, Spain was viewed by the rest of the world as a backward, insignificant place. The **Bourbon** dynasty replaced the Spanish kings during the **War of the Spanish Succession** and the English took **Gibraltar** in 1704. Spain fell under the influence of France for nearly a century and following the defeat of the Spanish fleet at the **Battle of Trafalgar** in 1805 off the coast of Cádiz, the French proceeded to ransack the country of its wealth and architectural treasures.

The French were finally driven out in the **War of Independence** in 1814, aided by Britain's Duke of Wellington, but little improved.

An era of coups and minor civil wars followed and the American colonies asserted their independence one by one, Cuba being the last to shake off Spanish rule in 1898.

The Twentieth Century

In 1923, **General Primo de Rivera** carried out a successful military coup and remained in power for six years, succeeding only in causing the peseta to collapse and compounding Spain's problems at a time of deepening world recession. The **Second Republic** was founded in 1931 and major social reforms were initiated to curb the strength of the wealthy landowners. But strikes and peasant rebellions continued, with widespread disillusionment caused by the reforms; some said they were too rapid, others indecisive.

Spain's problems intensified under the radical right-wing government that came to power in 1934 and proceeded to reverse all the reforms made by the previous government. By 1936, public opinion had swung again and the left took over, but nothing could

---

SPANISH POLICE

There are three types of police in Spain. In rural locations, the most prolific are the **Guardia Civil**, founded in 1848 by the Duque de Almhada to fight bandits in the countryside. Guardia Civil wear green uniforms with black tricorne hats and deal with traffic offences and law and order generally.

Smaller towns have a **Policía Municipal**, who wear navy blue and deal with local crimes and urban traffic control. They are funded by the town hall. Towns with a population of more than 20,000 have in addition a **Policía Nacional** force, funded by the government and armed with machine guns. The Policía Nacional, who wear navy blue, are responsible for dealing with serious crime on a nationwide basis.

be done to stop Spain sliding into total anarchy. In July of that year, **General Francisco Franco** led an army uprising against the socialist government and three years of bitter, bloody civil war between the Republicans and Loyalists and Franco's Nationalists followed. Support from Italy and Germany led to Franco's eventual victory and in 1939 he proclaimed himself head of state of an exhausted Spain.

Franco's Rule

Even harder times followed, with a mass exodus of Spaniards overseas. Thousands of republicans were imprisoned and executed and any legislation favouring the rights of peasants was revoked. Censorship was enforced and by the end of **World War II**, in which Spain remained neutral, the country was economically and politically isolated. Spain was ostracized by the United Nations and many countries cut off diplomatic relations. However, in the 1950s American loans were given in return for the right to establish nuclear bases in Spain. This kick-started the economy and created a new dawn on the Costa del Sol, an area earmarked for the development of package tourism.

Right: *General Francisco Franco's rule was a bleak period for many Spaniards.* **Opposite:** *Tourism is the mainstay of the economy on the Costa del Sol.*

The Costa del Sol Today

Massive investment in tiny fishing villages like **Marbella** and **Torremolinos** followed and the advent of charter flights in the 1960s brought the first plane loads of package tourists to the coast. Franco died in 1975, having nominated King Juan Carlos as his successor.

In 1982 the Socialist Worker's Party (PSOE), led by **Felipe Gonzáles**, was elected. Andalucía became an autonomous province in 1983 and in 1985, the border with Gibraltar was reopened. The socialist government successfully integrated Spain into the **European Community** in 1986 and the country continued to recover economically, putting itself in the world spotlight in 1992 with the **Expo** in Sevilla, the **Olympics** in Barcelona and **European City of Culture** in Madrid all happening in the same year.

HISTORICAL CALENDAR

25,000BC Cave dwellers in southern Spain leave primitive paintings in Nerja and La Pileta.
4000BC Neolithic tribes arrive from North Africa.
2500BC Dolmens constructed around what is now Antequera.
1100BC Phoenicians found the city of Cádiz.
500BC Carthaginians colonize southern Spain.
210BC Roman colonization begins after second Punic War. Málaga and Córdoba are important Roman cities. Andalucía is named Baetica.
AD400 Roman Empire in decline. Vandals from northern Europe inhabit Baetica and name it Vandalusía.
AD500 Vandals displaced by Visigoths, who found cities at Merida and Córdoba.
AD711 Moors from North Africa conquer Spain.

756 Abd-ar-Rahman I becomes first ruler of al-Andalus. Construction of Mezquita begun at Córdoba.
928 Abd-ar-Rahman III founds Caliphate of Córdoba.
1031 Caliphate splits into *taifas* – small kingdoms. Invasions from North Africa of Almoravids and Almohads re-establish Muslim authority.
1212 Christian victory at Las Navas de Tolosa (Jaén).
1492 Fall of Granada, last Moorish kingdom. All Jews and Arabs banished by Ferdinand and Isabella. Christopher Columbus reaches Caribbean.
1500 Golden Renaissance age of art and culture.
1609 Last of the Spanish Muslims expelled.
1700 War of Spanish Succession won by Felipe V, a Bourbon king.

1808 French occupation. Andalucía systematically divided into eight provinces.
1898 Cuba, Spain's last colony, is lost.
1923 Dictatorship of Primo de Rivera.
1936–39 Spanish Civil War and beginning of Franco dictatorship.
1962 First tourism development on Costa del Sol.
1975 Franco dies and the monarchy is restored.
1983 Andalucía votes to become one of Spain's 17 autonomous regions.
1985 Border with British Colony Gibraltar reopened.
1986 Spain joins EC.
1992 Expo in Sevilla and Olympic Games in Barcelona.
1999 Huge investment made in various tourism projects for the new Millennium.

Above: *The landmark Barqueta Bridge in Sevilla was built for Expo '92.*

GOVERNMENT AND ECONOMY

Spain today is a constitutional monarchy, ruled by **King Juan Carlos**, who is also commander-in-chief of the armed forces. The country comprises 50 provinces in 17 autonomous regions; Málaga, for example, is a province in the region of Andalucía, the capital of which is Sevilla. Economic and social problems continue to plague Andalucía, which despite its 'sunshine coast' and wealth of artistic treasures, is the poorest region of Spain with one of the highest rates of unemployment in the EU. The feudal system of wealthy landowners and oppressed workers has never really been abolished and much of the region's labour force has turned to tourism for its income. This, too, received a blow in the European recession of the early 1990s and the European tourism industry remains highly volatile today.

Investment in cleaning up the coast, however, and the blaze of publicity for Expo '92 in Sevilla, as well as the improvements in infrastructure it generated, provide hope for the future. The Costa del Sol has already acknowledged the environmental problems caused by the influx of mass tourism in the 1970s. What is important is that the coast now moves with the times to accommodate the more inquisitive, 'green' tourist of the new generation.

THE PEOPLE

The Costa del Sol is a genuinely cosmopolitan society, comprising a benevolent mix of expatriates and Spaniards. The expatriates, many of them retired from Britain and Germany, are attracted by the warm climate, abundant golf and bridge afternoons and the relatively high standard of living and actually outnumber Spaniards in some of the more attractive coastal villages such as **Mijas**. The locals, meanwhile, are easy-going and tolerant, many of them sustained financially by the annual tourist invasion which outnumbers them.

Having endured such a dramatic and at times devastating past, Andalucían people never miss an excuse to celebrate life, although this is often done by dramatizing death, through deep-seated rituals like the bullfight and flamenco music. Poverty is still a genuine issue and despite the improvements in the economy as a result of tourism, Andalucía still has Spain's highest rate of **unemployment** at over 25% in some areas. Having expressed this, there is no real resentment of the tourists and serious crime is not a threat; Andalucíans are proud and optimistic and even in the face of economic gloom will live life to the full.

Arabs inhabited al-Andalus for almost 800 years from the 8th to the 15th centuries and while today's growing Arab population, particularly around Marbella, simply enjoys the area's climate and lifestyle, the influence of the Moors of 500 years ago is everywhere – in architecture, place names, food, town plans and art.

Southern Spain also has a large **gypsy** population which has never really integrated into the mainstream. Gypsies follow their own traditions and tend to live in tight communities isolated from Spanish society. The downside of this is that they are less educated and as a result suffer high unemployment.

CELEBRITY-SPOTTING

While the heady days of the 1970s when the Costa del Sol was the most fashionable haunt of Europe's jet set have passed, the coast and Marbella in particular continue to attract celebrities and famous figures. **King Fahd of Saudi Arabia** has had a house built outside Marbella bearing a remarkable resemblance to the White House. Former James Bond **Sean Connery** has a home here, as does British chat show hostess **Cilla Black** and actor **Antonio Banderas** makes regular visits to his home town, Málaga. Sporting stars **Bjorn Borg**, **Franz Beckenbauer** and **Arantxa Sanchez Vicario** take holidays on the coast, as do **Shirley Bassey** and **Joan Collins**, frequenting star-studded hotels like the Marbella Club, itself founded by **Prince Hohenlohe of Liechtenstein**.

Below: *A farmer taking a break from his labours.*

CALENDAR OF FESTIVALS

January: Cabalgate de los Reyes Magos (Three Kings Parade), Málaga – parades of floats, with sweets distributed to children.
February: Carnaval – pre-Lenten festivity.
March: Semana Santa (Holy Week), Sevilla and Málaga – sombre, nightly candlelit processions during the week before Easter.
April: Feria de Abril (April Fair), Sevilla – bullfights, flamenco, equestrian events and street parties.
May: Feria del Caballo (Horse Fair), Jerez – highlight of the equestrian year.
June: 11: Corpus Christi – a national holiday with bullfights and fireworks.
July: 16: Virgen del Carmen – processions of boats celebrating the patroness of fishermen.
August: 9–19: Feria de Málaga (Fair of the South of Spain) – funfairs, circuses, bullfights, flamenco.
September: Feria de Ronda – highlight is the *corrida goyesca*, a costumed bull-fight. Fiesta de la Vindímia, Jerez – flamenco, parades and horse events following the wine harvest.
October: San Miguel fiesta in Granada.

Religion and Language

Some 97% of Spaniards are **Roman Catholic**, although there is no state religion and small communities of Protestants, Jews and Muslims exist. **Castilian Spanish** is spoken everywhere; the Basque, Catalan and Galician languages of the north are not heard in the south. On the Costa del Sol, **English** is widely understood.

Festivals

Every town in Spain has a patron saint, adding an important festival to the annual calendar. Dates of these vary but the main events take place in Estepona, Benalmádena, Torremolinos, Nerja and Fuengirola between July and October.

Every town's saint's day is celebrated by a *romería*, a pilgrimage to some holy spot outside the town where people spend the day celebrating in honour of their saint. Colourful gypsy wagons, flamenco dancers and riders in traditional attire parade through the streets, carrying an effigy of the saint in question, singing and passing round flagons of *sangria* and bottles of *fino*. Stalls along the way serve *tapas* and gradually, the whole town moves out to

Right: *Everybody dresses in traditional costume for the annual* romería.

the shrine for a night of barbecues, vast *paellas* cooked over an open fire, flamenco dancing and singing and dressage competitions. There are firework displays and sometimes a funfair and everybody dresses up in local costume, so it really is worth timing a visit to coincide with a local event.

The *Feria de Málaga* is the largest and most spectacular of the summer festivals, lasting for ten days in August, during which time theatrical events, funfairs, brilliant firework displays, bullfights, folk bands and tournaments spring up overnight.

Holy Week and the April Fair

Some festivals have a serious element and *Semana Santa*, or Holy Week, in Sevilla is slightly eerie, with sombre music and ornate floats depicting scenes from the Passion, accompanied by men in hooded outfits. Mournful *saetas* are sung and thousands of candles offer the only light. After Easter, the whole of Sevilla turns out for *Feria de Abril* (April Fair), a vast celebration of bullfights, flamenco, cultural events and drinking.

Jerez de la Frontera

The end of April brings *Feria del Caballo* (**Jerez Horse Fair**), a highlight of the equestrian year. Local breeders, reputed to rear the finest horses in Spain, show off their skills at competitive events and an enthusiastic audience enjoys sherry-tasting.

Vendimia (**wine festival**) in September follows the blessing of the grape harvest and includes flamenco dancing, bullfights, parades and more horse events.

Bullfighting

The bullfight, also known as the **Fiesta Brava**, **Los Toros** or **La Lidia**, is an ancient art steeped in ritual and is recorded as far back as 2000BC, in a wall painting excavated at Knossós in Crete depicting acrobats vaulting over the horns of a charging bull. The Visigoths who once inhabited Andalucía practised a primitive form of bullfighting but it was the Moors, almost 3000 years

Above: *Holy Week in Sevilla is one of Andalucía's more sombre festivals.*

USEFUL WORDS

Alcazaba ● Moorish castle or fortress
Alcázar ● Moorish fortified palace
Alameda ● promenade or park
Ayuntamiento ● town hall
Barrio ● quarter or suburb
Carretera ● main road
Corrida ● bullfight
Cueva ● cave
Judería ● Jewish quarter
Mirador ● lookout point
Mudéjar ● style of architecture produced by Moors under the Christians
Plaza de Toros ● bullring
Puerto ● port
Puerto deportivo ● marina
Reconquista ● Period between 8th–15th centuries when the Roman Catholics reconquered Moorish Spain, mainly in Andalucía

Right: *Bullfighting is taken very seriously in southern Spain and modern-day matadors can become millionaires.*
Opposite: *Golf courses line the western Costa del Sol and crowds are rare.*

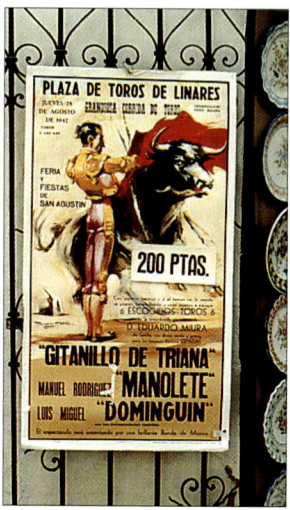

later, who turned the spectacle into an art form. It became more widespread in the late 18th century.

Love it or hate it, attending a *corrida* (bullfight) provides a valuable insight into the culture of Andalucía. The real stars of the ring can be seen in Sevilla and Córdoba, although Málaga, Estepona and Marbella all attract a knowledgeable and enthusiastic following.

A typical *corrida* involves three matadors and six bulls, massive fighting specimens which have been specially bred for their aggression. Each encounter will last about 15 minutes and forms three acts. The star of the show is the matador, expensively dressed in a *traje de lucas* (suit of lights) of an intricately embroidered silk jacket, black pants and a *montera*, a bicorne hat.

First, the bull is taunted with magenta capes swept in graceful arcs, before the *picadores* enter the ring mounted on horseback. Their job is to lance the bull's neck and weaken its muscles in preparation for the kill. Next, the *banderilleros*, who are on foot, drive brightly coloured steel darts into the bull's shoulders before the matador is finally alone in the ring with the bull for the final act, the *faena* or *la suerte de la muerte* (*muerte* means death). The matador works the crowd into a frenzy as he plays with the maddened bull using a small cape before moving in for the kill, in which he plunges his sword between the animal's shoulder blades. Matadors are national heroes and some become millionaires but most of them incur serious wounds during their careers and many pay with their lives.

MATADORS

Matadors are national heroes in Spain, contemporary stars often becoming multi-millionaires. A good matador will fight up to 100 *corridas* in a year and can expect to be gored on average once a season. There were exceptions: one of the greatest fighters of all time, **Pedro Romero**, who was born in 1784 in Ronda, went on to kill over 6000 bulls, never being gored and fighting into his eighties.

Costillares, his contemporary, perfected the fine art of fighting with a cape. Their flamboyant colleague, **Pepe-Hillo**, was less fortunate and died after his 26th goring.

Joselito, one of the greats of the 19th century, was also killed by a bull.

The most comprehensive account of bullfighting in Spain is probably Ernest Hemingway's book *Death in the Afternoon*, inspired by his great friend, the matador **Antonio Ordóñez**.

Sport and Recreation

The Costa del Sol is nicknamed 'Costa del Golf' but in fact has a huge variety of sports on offer, made all the more pleasant by almost constant sunshine, cooling sea breezes and low humidity.

Facilities for waterskiing and dinghy sailing are available from the sandy beaches between Málaga and Estepona and the windsurfing season runs from March to November. Boards and tuition are available at the hotels, although real aficionados should head west to Tarifa, self-styled windsurfing capital of Europe and mainland Spain's southernmost point, buffeted by Atlantic winds.

Scuba diving is not particularly spectacular on the Costa del Sol, although the crystal clear waters around the stony beaches of Nerja have a fair amount of marine life. Diving schools operate in Gibraltar and Almería, as well, Gibraltar being the site of several interesting wrecks.

Residents of the Costa del Sol are tennis-mad and there are some very smart clubs, as well as courts belonging to the many hotels. Clinics and courses are run at the Lew Hoad Campo de Tennis near Fuengiròla, Andalucía's most famous tennis school.

Few visitors take time to explore the mountains behind the coast in any depth but leaflets on hiking trails are available from the tourist board, covering the Sierra Nevada and the Serranía de Ronda. High in the Sierra Nevada, mountain huts provide shelter for overnight stops but elsewhere, the trails are little more testing than a pleasant meander through the pine forests. Hunting and fishing permits are available, the main game season extending from September to December. Mountain biking, cross country and downhill skiing, parapenting and paragliding are also growing in popularity in the Sierra Nevada.

> **TENNIS ON THE COSTA DEL SOL**
>
> When Wimbledon champion Lew Hoad opened his now-famous Campo de Tennis in Mijas in the 1970s, it was the only tennis club on the Costa del Sol. With so many up-and-coming Spanish tennis stars, the sport continues to grow in popularity and there are now over 20 clubs along the coast. The largest are at the **Hotel Atalaya Park** in Estepona (nine courts), **Club Internacional de Tenis**, San Pedro (11 courts), **Puente Romano Hotel**, Marbella (11 courts) **Club Hotel Los Monteros**, Marbella (10 courts), and the **Hotel Don Carlos**, Marbella (11 courts). The Spanish Tourist Board produces a useful leaflet, *Tennis on the Costa del Sol*, with full details.

Above: *Beach rides at sunset can be arranged from stables along the coast.*

Southern Spain is legendary for its beautiful Andalucían horses and riding in all forms, from trekking to high school dressage, is popular. **Horse-riding** is a relaxing way to enjoy the countryside and there are some excellent stables along the coast, offering beach rides at sunset and gentle treks through the hills, as well as specialist companies providing longer trails with overnight stops at small country hotels.

Flamenco

Impromptu flamenco under the stars on a hot summer's night, or in a smoky bar in the backstreets of Málaga is a primitive, magical experience which is far removed from the frills and castanets of the 'typical folklore' promoted in the tourist resorts.

Essentially an outlet for passion and unhappiness, good flamenco is a kind of spiritual bond between musicians, dancer and onlookers. As the raw emotion of the song, the hypnotic hand-clapping and finger-snapping of the audience and the fantastically fast stamping of the dancer build up into a cathartic finale, it is often accompanied by spontaneous shouts of encouragement and emotion.

Strands of many cultures have come together to form the music but it originates from the gypsies of **Sevilla**,

Jerez and **Cádiz** in the 19th century who sang mournful laments of lost love and oppression. Elements of the music come from **North Africa**, **India**, **Greece**, **Egypt** and **Pakistan** but the result is pure Andalucía.

Flamenco became part of civilized society in the 19th century as café entertainment and its raw intensity was diffused slightly as it began to be integrated into popular folklore music. The *sevillana* is one of the most popular forms, celebrated at Andalucía's many summer festivals and popular among young people, most of whom know the basic steps. This is the only form of flamenco where castanets are used, contrary to popular belief, and elsewhere visitors are expected to join in with *palmadas* (hand clapping) and *pitos* (finger snapping) to create staccato counter-rhythms to the drumming of the dancer's feet. Male roles have more emphasis on footwork, while female dancers demonstrate body and hand movements that are both dramatic and graceful. Their brilliantly coloured dresses are cut higher at the front to show off the skill in the steps.

Flamenco is used to express joy as well as agony and there are three levels of intensity: *grande* or *jondo* (deep); *intermedio*, much less profound and sometimes almost oriental-sounding; and *pequeno* or *canto chico*, a lighter, more joyful form. The dances include *tango*, *fandango*, *farruca* and *zambra*, although everything is improvised within a repertoire of fixed rhythms. A point to note is that the guitarist follows the dancer, not the other way round and *duende*, the moment of total understanding between musician, dancer and *aficionados*, is achieved when the three are completely immersed in the music and dance.

The visitor's best chance of finding good flamenco is to join in with a local *feria*, where talented travelling artistes often perform. The local tourist office will give some advice on the best *café cantates*; most are located in the backstreets of Málaga and Sevilla.

Below: *'Real' flamenco is worth seeking out in the backstreets of Málaga and Sevilla.*

Art and Architecture

For centuries a centre of art, culture and learning, Andalucía's heritage is rich and exciting, with some of the world's most beautiful **Islamic** monuments within reach of the Costa del Sol.

The first remnants of note dates back to **Roman** times – the ruins of Italica near Sevilla and the magnificent bronze of a Roman youth in the museum at Antequera. But it was the Moors, who arrived in AD711, who made the biggest architectural impact on the region, establishing themselves in Córdoba and building **La Mezquita**, a mosque that was regarded as one of the wonders of the world in its time. Having come from Damascus, centre of the Islamic world, the Moors introduced intricate Arabic calligraphy, brilliantly coloured mosaics and structures like **La Giralda** minaret and the **Torre de Oro**, a tower tiled in gold in Sevilla. In Granada, the last Moorish kingdom of al-Andalus, **La Alhambra** represents the pinnacle of Moorish culture, palaces of ornate stuccos and exquisitely carved wooden ceilings set among serene gardens and fountains.

The *reconquista* allowed Moorish architecture to continue but with modifications. Gothic and Islamic styles were blended under the Christians to create **Mudéjar**, vividly illustrated in the **Alcázar** (palace) in Sevilla. Then, in the 15th century, austere **Gothic**, the style of Sevilla's massive cathedral, evolved into **Plateresque**, with ostentatious use of gold and silver from the New World to adorn every available surface, as in the **Capilla Real** (Royal Chapel) in Granada.

Renaissance style arrived in the mid-16th century, one of the finest examples being the **Palacio de Carlos V** in the Alhambra at Granada, strangely utilitarian among the intricate arches and pillars. In the 17th and 18th centuries, architectural style swung back to the opulence of **Baroque**. An early example is Granada's cathedral, the façade of which was completed by painter Alonso Cano in 1664.

Opposite: *Sevilla's Giralda Tower is one of the most spectacular examples of Moorish architecture in Spain.* **Left:** *In contrast, new landmarks built for Expo '92 are strikingly modern.*

Fine Art

Most of the work of painters who lived or spent time in southern Spain is in Madrid's **Prado** museum although some pieces remain in Sevilla and Málaga. The sacristy of Granada's **Capilla Real** has a valuable collection of 15th-century Flemish art belonging to Queen Isabella, including work by **Memling**, **Bouts** and **Van der Weyden**, as well as a small **Botticelli**.

Art flourished in Andalucía in the 17th century: **Velázquez** (1599–1660) was born in Sevilla, although he left the south aged 24; **Francisco de Zurbarán** (1598–1664) arrived in Sevilla in 1628 and **Bartolomé Esteban Murillo** (1618–1682) and **José Ribera** (1591–1652) worked here. Pieces by all three are housed in the Museo de Bellas Artes in Sevilla and in the cathedral, there's a beautiful **Goya** (1746–1828): the story of Santa Rufina and Santa Justa.

With the exception of Goya, who painted scenes from the Plaza de Toros in Ronda, the 18th and 19th centuries were a bleak period culturally for Andalucía. **Picasso** (1881–1973) was born in Málaga but left for Barcelona at an early age – Málaga's Museo de Bellas Artes has a selection of his early sketches alongside some **Murillos** and **Riberas** and some fine sculptures.

PARADORES

Paradores is a government-run chain of hotels in historic or beautiful locations and offer the visitor the opportunity to stay in a castle or palace at reasonable rates.

The first *parador* was developed in 1926 under the supervision of King Alfonso XIII and today there are 85 in the chain, including seven on or near the Costa del Sol. Paradors are divided into three categories: **natural**, **coastal** or **monumental** setting. *Paradores* along the Costa del Sol include: Parador de Málaga Gibralfaro; Parador de Granada, located inside the Alhambra; Arcos de la Frontera, in a dramatic clifftop location and Ronda, overlooking the gorge. Modern *paradores* are located at Torremolinos, Nerja and Antequera.

Right: Tapas *are snacks but are often filling enough to constitute a meal.*

CHEESE

Traditionally eaten as a *tapa*, cheese occasionally appears at the end of meals accompanied by quince jelly. Most of the local cheeses are made of goat's milk, sometimes blended with sheep's milk and do not travel well, which is why they are not exported.

Look out for the fresh, cylindrical goat's cheese of the Alpujarras and Sierra Nevada and the stronger, yellow Ronda cheese, preserved in olive oil. Grazalema produces a unique sheep's cheese, cured for several months and preserved in vats of olive oil. **Queso de Cádiz** is a general term for the semi-cured goat's cheese from the mountains, yellow in colour and quite strong to taste. **Valle de los Pedrojes** is a sheep's cheese from around Córdoba. One of the most popular cheeses, the hard, tangy **Manchego**, comes from La Mancha, the province next to Almería.

Food and Drink

Andalucían cuisine is tremendously varied, ranging from fresh seafood and colourful vegetable dishes to rich, meaty stews from the mountains. Preparation is relatively simple and flavours are strong, with widespread use of garlic, cumin (which has been around since the Moors lived in Andalucía), extra virgin olive oil and spicy marinades.

Tapas

The *tapas* bar has turned out to be one of Spain's most popular exports in recent years. This habit of consuming several small dishes with a glass of *fino*, the pale, dry sherry from Jerez, before dinner is an essential part of the Spanish working day. Because of the heat, Spaniards enjoy a long, late lunch followed by a *siesta* (rest) and work quite late into the evening. It is then customary to go for a stroll and have a few drinks accompanied by enough *tapas* to stave off any hunger until supper, which is usually as late as 22:00.

'*Tapa*' actually means 'lid' and its origin is the little plates of **snacks** bartenders used to place over drinks. Some bars, usually those frequented by local people, serve free *tapas* at the bar, often something simple like bowls of **olives**, slices of *jamón serrano* – cured mountain ham – and plates of **salted almonds**.

Elsewhere, a selection of *tapas* dishes is enough for an evening meal for most people. Specialities of the Costa del Sol include *pescaito frito* (small fish fried in batter), spicy *chorizo* sausages, *champiñones al ajillo* (mushrooms baked in garlic), *queso* (cubes of smoked cheese), red peppers in olive oil and *tortilla* (Spanish omelette filled with potato and onion and served cold in slices).

Look out for *calamares* (tiny, marinated squid) and *canaillas* (miniature sea snails), which are regarded as a great delicacy. Offal is popular in this part of the world and small pieces of liver cooked with onion and spices is another favourite. All this should be washed down by a glass of chilled *fino*.

Regional Specialities

Andalucía is the home of *gazpacho*, a thick, cold soup made from tomatoes, onion, bread, cumin, lemon juice and vast quantities of fresh garlic. Usually served with diced green pepper, chopped hard-boiled egg and fried croutons, *gazpacho* is a meal in itself.

Another traditional **cold soup**, originating from Málaga and perfect for summer, is *ajo blanco*, made with almonds and garlic and served chilled with fresh grapes. When the weather is cooler, try *sopa de pescado*, an all-encompassing term for **fish soup**, seasoned with tomato, onion, garlic and brandy.

Fish, not surprisingly, is the principal speciality of the coast. On some beaches, fishermen still cook fresh sardines on skewers over an open fire. In restaurants, fish is served marinated or fried, ranging from *calamares en su tinta* – tiny squid cooked in its own ink – to *gambas con ajillo*, giant prawns in garlic. Look out for *pez espada* (swordfish), *rape* (monkfish) and *bonito* (tuna), all of which are caught locally and served grilled, brushed with olive oil and seasoning.

ANDALUCIAN IMPORTS

Many of the ingredients that make up the gastronomic specialities of southern Spain are not native to the region. Phocian Greeks brought **olives** and **vines** around 1000BC and the Moors, hundreds of years later, introduced **pepper**, **cumin** **cinnamon** and **coriander**. The conquering of the Americas brought hitherto unknown foods like **maize**, **potatoes**, **tomatoes** and, of course, **tobacco**.

Below: *Sardines roasted on skewers in the sand are a typical sight on the beaches of Torremolinos.*

Above: *Spicy chorizo sausages and pungent cheeses are good buys in the markets along the coast.* **Opposite:** *Sherry is presented with a flourish at tastings in the bogedas.*

Inland, traditional dishes incorporate the **game**, **freshwater fish** and **wild herbs** of the mountains. Casseroles are prepared using **rabbit** or **hare** cooked in white wine and a speciality of the Cádiz region, west of the Costa del Sol, is *pastel de pichones*, or **pigeon pâté**. In the Alpujarras, in Granada province, a speciality is mountain **trout** stuffed with cured ham. One of the most widespread meat dishes is *rabo de torro* – **oxtail** prepared with tomatoes, onions and spices. Some recipes are not for the squeamish, particularly around Granada where brains, intestines and bulls' testicles form the basis of a couple of specialities, *tortilla Sacromonte* and *revoltillos*.

Vegetarians will not starve, however. Salads in Andalucía are quite delicious: crisp lettuce, succulent olives and huge, sweet tomatoes drizzled with olive oil, with variations including artichoke, fresh asparagus and chopped eggs. Vegetable dishes include *espinaces con ajillo* (spinach with garlic), *garbanzos con espinaces* (chickpeas with spinach) and *judias verdes con salsa de tomate* (green beans with tomato sauce and fresh garlic).

Sherry

Andalucía's most famous wine comes from a small area around the town of **Jerez de la Frontera** which forms one corner of the 'sherry triangle' with El Puerto de Santa María and Sanlúcar de Barrameda in the province of Cádiz, a couple of hours' drive inland from the Costa del Sol. The climate, salty sea air, chalky soil and generations of expertise produces the world's finest *fino*, the dry, pale gold sherry drunk chilled all over Andalucía with *tapas*.

The name 'sherry' is an anglicized version of the name of the town **Jerez**, which in turn is a corruption of the Moorish name *Xerez*. The Phoenicians were the original

---

SPANISH PRONUNCIATION

a	short as in *cat*
e	short as in *pet*
i	long, like *e* in *be*
o	long, as in *note*
u	long as in *flute* and silent after *q*, *gue*- and *gui*-
v	in the middle of a word is pronounced *b*
c	before the vowel *i* or *e* is pronounced either *s* or *th* – more often an *s* sound
g	before the vowel *i* or *e* is pronounced like *ch* in *loch*
j	as in *loch*
ll	as in *million*
ñ	as in *canyon*
z	*th* or *s* in Andalucía

wine-growers in the area, followed by the Romans, who exported wine from Jerez all over their empire. After the *reconquista* drove out the Moors and Jews, British firms established *bodegas* in the area and to this day, **Britain** remains the biggest export market, consuming some 70% of all sherry exported from Spain.

In addition to *fino*, there are three other types of sherry drunk in Spain. *Manzanilla* is a type of dry *fino* with a salty tang, acquired from the area around Sanlúcar de Barrameda and a perfect accompaniment to the seafood in which the area specializes. *Amontillado*, meanwhile, is a more pungent wine that has been aged beyond its normal span in the *bodega* (wine cellar), while *Oloroso*, the heaviest style of sherry, is usually sweetened and sold as cream exclusively to the British market.

Wine

Most of Spain's famous wine-producing areas are in the north but the area immediately behind the Costa del Sol does grow some wine of its own. Málaga has its own *Denominacion de Origen* growing mainly **Moscatel** and **Pedro Ximenez** grapes producing dark, sweet wines.

Wine in supermarkets and restaurants along the Costa del Sol is exceptionally good value and while they may not be local, names to look out for include **Campo Viejo** (fruity reds and dry whites), **Marqués de Caceres** (red *Riojas* and oak-aged whites) and **Torres** (fruity, aromatic whites like Viña Sol and Esmerelda and soft, fresh reds). **Cava** is sparkling wine made by the champagne method and the two biggest producers are **Codorníu** and **Freixenet**. Andalucía is also Spain's biggest brandy producer, mainly from the sherry *bodegas* around Jerez.

One drink every visitor is likely to encounter is *sangria*, a concoction of chilled red wine, citrus fruits, lemonade, brandy and ice, drunk by Spaniards at barbecues and picnics. *Sangria* is very refreshing and its easy, drinkable quality means some tourists consume it to excess, underestimating its potency.

2
Málaga

Málaga, provincial capital and the second largest city in Andalucía after Sevilla, has made relatively few concessions to tourism and is refreshingly Spanish, with fascinating old buildings tucked in among the high-rise blocks, leafy parks and gardens and tiny bars in back streets where old men gossip over a *fino* and *tapas*.

Málaga has a long and chequered history. The city was founded by **Phoenicians** in the eighth century BC who called it **Malaka**. Subsequent Carthaginian and Roman rulers developed Malaka into a busy port before Moorish armies from Islamic Africa invaded Spain in AD711.

The Moors were quick to build the **Alcazaba**, the fortified castle on top of Gibralfaro hill and Málaga continued its role as the port of Granada for some 700 years. In 1487, the city fell to the Catholic kings after a bitter siege, following which the Moors were persecuted and stripped of their possessions.

For several centuries, Málaga fell into decline, revived briefly in the early 1800s by development of the wine-growing industry and sugar production from the cane plantations along the **Costa Tropical** to the east. But Málaga entered into a decline again early in this century when a plague destroyed the vines and, much later, the city's monuments were bombed and destroyed during the Spanish Civil War.

Only in the last 50 years have Málaga's fortunes turned around. Largely untouched by the Costa del Sol's tourism boom to the west, the city underwent a facelift in the early 1990s, restoring its beaches and promenade.

DON'T MISS

*** Antequera: an ancient, beautiful city packed with architectural gems.
** Málaga: do a walking tour of the old part and its historic sights.
** El Torcal: some of Europe's most spectacular rock formations.
** Garganta del Chorro and the **Lake District:** deep gorges, cool, green pine forests and magnificent mountain scenery.
* Jardin de la Concepción: a beautiful tropical garden of rare specimens set among fountains and waterfalls.

Opposite: *The Costa del Sol stretches away into the haze beyond Málaga's roof-tops.*

CLIMATE

Spring and autumn are the best times to enjoy the city on foot; July, August and September are simply too hot for walking with midday temperatures well over 30°C (86°F). Late spring is also the best time to appreciate the varied flora and fauna around El Torcal and El Chorro. Málaga is also pleasantly mild in winter, although trips to higher ground inland, including El Torcal, are limited by snow and chilling winds during January and February.

City Sightseeing

By far the best way to explore Málaga's centre is on foot as the traffic is always busy. Everything shuts down for *siesta* between 13:00 and 17:00, so early morning or early evening is the best time to explore.

Gibralfaro ★★★

A walk up the Gibralfaro hill rising high above the city gives a superb perspective of the centre and its fortified **Alcazaba** sprawling below, with views of the port and the Costa del Sol stretching away to the west. A footpath from the **Ayuntamiento** (town hall) winds up through pinewoods and tropical gardens to the 14th-century **Moorish castle** with its solid walls and parapets and the Moorish lighthouse which gave the hill its name – *Jebel al Faro*, or hill of the lighthouse (open daily 09:30–20:00). Málaga's small *parador* (state-run hotel) enjoys spectacular panoramic views from just below the castle. At the foot of the hill is the 19th-century bullring, where Sunday *corridas* attract big crowds and big names.

English Cemetery ★

A short walk east of the bullring is the English Cemetery (open daily 09:30–13:00, 14:30–17:30). Founded in 1830 by Britain's Consul-General, William Mark, it was used to provide proper Christian burials for Protestants who died on Spanish soil during a period when non-Catholics were considered to be infidels. Here you can explore the tombstone inscriptions, many of them dating back 150 years, and written in English.

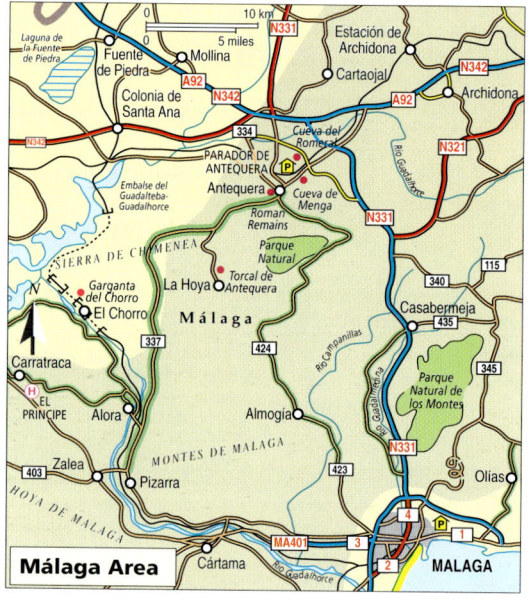

Málaga Area

Alcazaba ***

From the bullring, walk along **Paseo del Parque** through gardens of palms, bougainvillea and exotic shrubs, past the cream and brown neo-Baroque **Ayuntamiento** built in 1919. **Plaza de Aduana**, the square of the old Customs House, forms the entrance to the Alcazaba, a massive fortress started by the Moors in the eighth century and finished in the 11th (open Monday–Saturday 10:00–13:00, 17:00–20:00; Sunday 10:00–14:00). Just outside the Alcazaba is a Roman theatre, excavated in the early 1950s and the only visible Roman structure left in the city.

A cobbled path winds up through luxuriant gardens within the castle walls to an 11th-century palace, now housing the city's small **Archaeological Museum** which includes fragments of pottery from Roman times as well as mosaics and artefacts found locally.

Cathedral **

A short walk along the Paseo del Parque and up Calle de Molina Lario is Málaga's cathedral, built on the site of an old mosque and still unfinished, giving it the local name **La Manquita**, or 'the one-armed lady'. Money ran out in 1782 and as a result, the cathedral has only one tower. Despite this, it has been declared a national monument. Inside, the altar is made of Italian marble, with agate columns, and the intricate 17th-century choir stall was carved by **Pedro de Mena**, one of Andalucía's best known craftsman of the time.

CONVENT CAKES

A good deal of the cakes for which Andalucía is famous are made by ñuns, who support their convents by running small cake shops. The tradition stems from the sherry *bodegas* around Jerez, which would use egg whites in the clarification of their wines and give the yolks to the nuns. The influence of the Moors is strong, with widespread use of honey and almonds to create rich, very sweet delicacies.

Málaga has three such establishments: the abbey of **Santa Ana**, which specializes in *dulce de membrillo* – quince jelly; **Convento de las Clarisas**, selling quince jelly, coconut balls and lemon turnovers and the monastery of **Asunción**, famous for its *tortas de polverón*, little cakes with almonds and coconut biscuits. On Calle Larios, the main shopping street, the Casa Mira is the city's best known cake shop, selling Málaga sponge cake with raisins, fried doughnuts and *yemas*, traditional cakes made of egg yolk and sugar.

PICASSO

Pablo Picasso was born in Málaga in 1881. He painted his first picture at the age of 10 and by 15 had qualified for a place at the Barcelona School of Fine Art. During his career, he produced over 20,000 paintings, sketches and sculptures. One of his most important works illustrating contemporary Spanish history is *Guernica*, in honour of the Basque town bombed by the Germans. It is in Madrid's museum of 20th-century art.

Casa Natal de Picasso ★

Picasso fans will no doubt want to see the place where the great artist was born. A few blocks northeast of the cathedral is the **Plaza de la Merced** (Our Lady of Mercy Square). Picasso's birthplace is on the north side of this leafy 18th-century square, which was once a market outside the city walls, situated in the **Casas de Campos** (open Monday–Friday 11:00–14:00 and 17:00–20:00, but mornings only in summer).

Today, the house holds the **Picasso Foundation**, managed by the Town Council. The foundation is a centre for research into and exhibition of contemporary art, including works by Picasso. This is not a place to see great works of art, but it does give a good insight into the artist's early life and influences.

1. Auana
2. Alcazaba
3. Archaeological Museum
4. Ayuntamiento
5. El Corte Inglés
6. Episcopal Palace
7. Estatua MA Heredia
8. Estatua Marques de Lacios
9. Iglesia de Santiago
10. Iglesia del Sagrario
11. Museo de Artes Tradiciones Populares
12. Palacio de Villalcazar
13. Picasso's Birthplace
14. Plaza de la Constitución
15. Teatro Romano

Museo de Artes y Tradiciones Populares *

West of the city on the bank of the Guadal-mina River, in a 17th-century coaching inn, this museum gives an insight into life before tourism on the Costa del Sol, with a wood-burning oven, an old *bodega*, or wine cellar, fishing and farming implements and a collection of popular ceramics among its exhibits. Open 10:00–13.00, 16:00–19:00 in winter, 10:00–13.30, 17:00–20:00 in summer, closed Saturday evenings and Sundays.

Finca La Concepción **

On the outskirts of Málaga, off the N331 Antequera road, is a botanical adventure. Finca La Concepción is a living museum of **exotic plants** and an ideal ramble for a hot day, set among fountains, Roman statues and waterfalls around a 19th-century mansion with a gazebo. A trail marked through the gardens with glazed tiles takes the visitor past the most interesting specimens including rare palms, cascading wisteria, magnolias, giant araucaria trees, Australian mimosa, eucalyptus and pine.

Above: The Immaculate Conception *by Batoleme Esteban Murillo (1617–82) in the Museo de Bellas Artes, Sevilla.*

Shopping and Nightlife

Three main streets – **Molina Lario**, **Calle de Marqués de Larios** and **Calle de Granada** – are lined with shops, boutiques, bars and cafés. The **Mercado Afarazanas**, the central market with a magnificent Moorish arch at its centre, is a riot of local colour, with fish, herbs, vegetables and tropical fruits from the coast on sale daily.

Málaga's best *tapas* bars are clustered in the streets around the cathedral and north of the **Alameda** (park). These are the places to try the sweet Málaga wine and fried fish, the local speciality, assorted seafood caught the same day and tossed in a deliciously light batter and deep fried. The atmospheric **Antigua Casa** on the **Alameda** is lined with barrels of sweet wine and is a popular place with the locals for a mid-morning *fino* and shellfish *tapas*.

> **COMMON CULINARY TERMS**
>
> *A la plancha* • grilled
> *al ajillo* • in garlic
> *asado* • roast or barbecued
> *astofado* • stewed
> *a la marinera* • cooked in wine with garlic and parsley
> *al horno* • baked
> *frito* • fried
> *pescados* • fish
> *mariscos* • seafood
> *revueltos, or huevos revueltos* • scrambled eggs, often served with asparagus, mushrooms or ham

NORTH OF MALAGA
Garganta del Chorro **

Northwest of Málaga, about an hour's drive on the N337, the road begins to climb up to the hillside village of **Alora**, overlooked by an imposing Moorish castle. From here, the scenery changes rapidly from rolling farmland to vast rock overhangs and precarious hairpin bends as the road follows a riverbed through pine forests, climbing all the time.

Over millions of years, the river has carved a sheer-sided gorge, the **Garganta del Chorro**, (El Chorro) through the limestone mountain and the view from the road is breathtaking. A rickety, wooden walkway clings to the rock face about halfway up and joins an extremely flimsy-looking bridge spanning the narrow gorge. The whole structure is called **El Camino del Rey** after King Alfonso XIII walked on it when he opened the Guadalhorce hydroelectric dam in 1921, but today it is extremely dangerous as the handrail is missing in several sections. A walk through the gorge to the other side is possible but only for those with a head for heights.

Beyond **El Chorro Gorge** is some of the most surprising scenery of this region; beautiful blue lakes fringed with sandy beaches and pine woods. This is the **Parque de Ardales**, a protected area created by ICONA, Spain's environmental agency, and is an ideal spot for a picnic. The lakes are actually reservoirs, blocked by a series of dams like the one below **El Chorro**. Campsites and *miradors* (lookout points) are clearly marked and there are a couple of good restaurants for lunch, including El Mirador which lives up to its name and has a scenic, peaceful outlook over the water.

GOLDEN EAGLE

The golden eagle has always been regarded as a symbol of courage and power, because of its size, aerial skills and the inaccessibility of its nesting sites. The female, the larger of the two sexes, grows up to 1m (3ft) in length, with a wingspan of over 2m (7ft). Roman myths associated the bird with Jupiter, king of the gods, and it became the emblem of many Roman legions, as well as the symbol of Germany and of the Austrian empire centuries later. The eagle nests on cliff edges and feeds on mammals ranging from mice to small deer. During the breeding season, eagles will kill other birds to feed to their young.

Parque Nacional El Torcal de Antequera **

Just outside Antequera is an extraordinary natural phenomenon. Millions of years of blasting by wind and water have eroded a whole mountain-top into bizarre, twisted shapes, now protected as one of the best preserved examples of karst, or limestone scenery, in Europe.

Named **El Torcal**, the whole area has been designated a national park and there are three walking trails for visitors to explore, wandering between fantasy rock formations that look like a stack of plates one minute and a human figure the next. Green markers indicate a gentle 45-minute stroll; orange one hour and red up to three hours and it is essential to stick to the path, as it's too easy to get lost in this strange moonscape.

In addition to the geology, the area has some interesting **flora** and **fauna**. To be precise, there are 11 species of reptile; 82 types of bird; 22 kinds of mammal, including wild cats, ferrets, foxes and rabbits. Look out for eagles, falcons and hawks above and salamander, snakes and tarantula below, as well as delicate Alpine flowers and orchids peeping between the rocks. A free audiovisual show at the visitors centre explains the formation of El Torcal and, downstairs, there's a working display of the geological process.

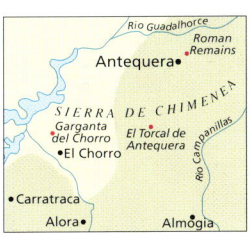

Good walking boots and a warm sweater are essential for these trails – the terrain is very uneven and the temperature a good 12C° (54F°) lower than down on the plain. In the winter months the rocks are even more inhospitable and dangerous, usually covered with a blanket of snow.

FUENTE DE PIEDRA

A short drive north of Antequera on the N334 is an unusual sight: a breeding colony of 10,000 pairs of **greater flamingo**. Every spring these birds form a sea of pink across the **Laguna de Fuente de Piedra**, a shallow lake with highly saline water which forms Europe's only inland breeding ground for the species. In three hours, it is possible to walk round the lake, past reed beds and marshes which sustain a wide variety of birdlife. Head out of town to the north on the MA454 and turn left at km6, at the Cortijo de la Herriaza. From here, a track follows the water's edge all the way back to Fuente de Piedra. Spring is the best time to visit.

Opposite: *In 1921, King Alfonso XIII actually walked along this precarious walkway.* **Left:** *Wind- and weather-blasted rocks form bizarre shapes at El Torcal.*

LOVERS' ROCK

This sad tale of ill-fated love is supposed to be true. In the Middle Ages, a young Christian from Antequera fell in love with a Moorish girl, a union which was strictly forbidden. The two fled on horseback, pursued by Moorish soldiers, until they reached the rock, which sticks up from the Antequera plain like the face of a huge sleeping giant. Rather than surrender, they climbed the rock and jumped to their deaths from the top.

ANTEQUERA

This charming 5000-year-old city is an architectural gem, with fascinating examples of architecture from Romans, Moors, Christians and even Neolithic Man. An easy hour's drive north of Málaga, Antequera can easily be combined with a visit to El Torcal.

Some of the oldest **dolmens** – prehistoric tombs – in Europe have been found here, and there are three around the city's northern outskirts open to the public, the most impressive of which is **Cueva de Menga** (open Tuesday–Friday 10:00–14:00, 15:00–17:30; Saturday–Sunday 10:00–14:00, entry free). How the huge rocks were cut and dragged into place to form crude caves remains a mystery, similar to that of Stonehenge in the UK.

Antequera is a mass of red-tiled roofs punctuated by some 30 church spires best admired from the Moorish **Alcazabar** which overlooks the city and the plain beyond. The gardens of the ruined Alcazabar are being restored and alleys of tall cypresses planted, framing magnificent views out across the chequered plains.

Palacio de Nájera ★★

The square bell-tower of the 18th-century **Palacio de Nájera** houses the small but rich **Museo Municipal** (open Tuesday–Saturday 10:00–13:30). It contains a striking bronze sculpture of a Roman boy, dating back to the first century AD and said to be one of the most important pieces of its kind ever to be found in Spain. A peasant stumbled on it in a field one day and his plough cut off the thumb of the right hand, but otherwise the statue is intact.

The museum also houses a remarkable collection of gold and silverware, belonging to the various orders of monks that have inhabited the city over the years. In complete contrast, the ground floor gallery contains a collection of the work of **Cristobál Toral**, an Antequeran artist whose almost three-dimensional, contemporary paintings are exhibited all over the world.

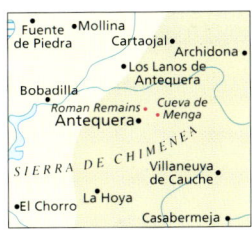

Opposite: *Lovers' Rock rises out of the plains beyond Antequera.*
Left: *Some of the best views of Antequera's spires are from the Alcazabar.*

Nuestra Señora del Carmen **

Antequera is known as a 'city of spires' and the most important, the **Church of El Carmen**, has been designated a national monument. A former convent and an unimposing Baroque structure from the outside, the church contains a magnificent 12m-high (40ft) wooden altar, built in the middle of the 18th century and covered with gilt in parts but crammed with intricate carvings of angels and saints. The whole surface of the church inside is adorned with brilliant colours.

Plaza de Toros **

The town has an attractive bullring, the only one in Spain to have a restaurant inside its walls. Underneath the tiered seating, try Antequera specialities such as *porra*, a paste of breadcrumbs, tomato and virgin olive oil filled with tuna flakes, dried ham and hard boiled eggs; and *Boquerones al a bonito*, fried anchovies stuffed with tuna. The *rabo de torro*, or oxtail, is voted by Spaniards as the best in Andalucía. Upstairs, there's a small **bullfighting museum** of stuffed bulls' heads and photos of some of the great matadors of yesteryear, as well as some ornate, sequined and brocaded costumes.

Málaga at a Glance

BEST TIMES TO VISIT

Málaga receives visitors year-round, broadly split into golfers in **winter** and holiday-makers in **summer**. July to September is too hot for most people to enjoy walking in the city and December to February can be cloudy. In spring – **March** to **May** – the city is at its greenest, as are the plains of Antequera and the national parks of El Torcal and Garganta del Chorro. From **September** to **November**, after the harvest, the countryside is usually rather dry and barren and consequently less photogenic. El Torcal is windy and snowy in winter; spring is the best time to enjoy the wildflowers.

GETTING THERE

Málaga International Airport has daily connections to many European and most other Spanish cities with **Iberia** and also **Air Europa**, tel: (95) 204-8249. Málaga's train station **(RENFE)** also has daily services to and from all the major cities in Spain, tel: (95) 231-2500. The drive from Madrid, motorway all the way, takes about 6½ hours. **Traffic information** is on tel: (91) 535-2222.

GETTING AROUND

Most of the major **car hire** companies and several local ones have offices at Málaga Airport (see above). Beware of parking illegally in the city as clamping and on-the-spot fines are rife. Never leave anything valuable in a car. The **electric train** is also an excellent option from the airport into the city. Local **bus services** in Spain are operated privately and most of the coastal routes are run by the **Portillo** bus company, tel: (95) 236-0191. Keep small change handy and pay on the bus. Buses run to Antequera but to reach El Torcal and Garganta del Chorro, a private car is the best option.

WHERE TO STAY

Málaga
LUXURY
Parador de Málaga-Gibralfaro, S/N 29016 Málaga, tel: (95) 222-1902, fax: (95) 222-1904. The best views in Málaga from the top of the Gibralfaro hill in the old Arab Alcazaba. Attractive, rustic building forming part of the *parador* chain.
Hotel Málaga Palacio, Cortina de Muelle 1, tel: (95) 221-5181. Four-star city hotel with pool and gardens; easy access to shops and sights.
Parador de Málaga-del Golf, Apartado de Correos 324-29080 Málaga, tel: (95) 238-1255, fax: (95) 238-8963. Modern *parador* on the beach, close to airport. Spacious grounds with very good 18-hole golf course and golf school.

MID-RANGE
Hotel Bahia de Málaga, Somera 8 – 29001 Málaga, tel: (95) 222-4305, fax: (95) 222-4303. Small and intimate city centre hotel with convenient parking facilities.
Hotel Los Naranjos, Paseo de Sancha, 35 – 29016 Málaga, tel: (95) 222-4317, fax: (95) 222-5975. A small hotel in a lively area, quite close to Gibralfaro.

BUDGET
Hotel del Sur, Trinidad Grund 13 – 29001 Málaga, tel: (95) 222-4803, fax: (95) 221-2416. Quiet hotel south of the Alameda gardens.
Hotel Niza, Larios 2 – 29001 Málaga, tel: (95) 222-7704. Small, one-star hotel in one of the main shopping streets.

Antequera
Parador de Antequera, Garcia del Olmo S/N – 29200 Antequera, tel: (95) 284-0901, fax: (95) 284-1312. A whitewashed *parador* with a swimming pool, situated in the quiet area of town.

Carratraca
Hostal El Principe, Antonio Rioboo 11, Carratraca, Málaga, tel: (95) 245-8020, fax: (95) 245-8101. This is a character-filled *hostal* in the palace built by King Ferdinand II. Bargain rates in luxury surroundings as only one room has private facilities. Bar and restaurant for guests.

Málaga at a Glance

El Chorro and El Torcal National Park

Camping in nearby Parque Ardales or rooms in local village only.

WHERE TO EAT

Málaga is famous for its fish restaurants and almost everywhere serves fried fish. *Tapas* bars are found all around the market, cathedral and **Alameda** (park) areas and are busy from about mid-morning onwards. Inland, dishes are more specialized and game and ham are a big feature.

Málaga
Parador de Málaga-Gibralfaro S/N 29016 Málaga, tel: (95) 222-1902, fax: (95) 222-1904. (*see* Where to Stay) Creative game cooking in addition to excellent fish dishes with romantic views of the city.

Bar Lo Gueno, Marin Garcia 9, Málaga. Lively, fashionable bar/restaurant with wide range of *tapas* and *raciones*, hams and cheeses.

Antigua Casa de Guardia, Alameda 18, Málaga, tel: (95) 221-4680. Local legend, serves seafood *tapas* to a lively crowd. Wine is served from wooden barrels behind the bar.

Antonio Martin, Plaza de la Malaguete, S/N, tel: (95) 222-7382. Historic seafront restaurant specializing in fish. There is a terrace in summer, log fire in winter.

El Cabra, C/Menita 20, Málaga, tel: (95) 229-1595. This well-known seafood restaurant is situated on the waterfront.

Antequera
La Espuela, Paseo Maria Cristina S/N Plaza de Toros, 29200 Antequera, tel: (95) 270-2633, fax: (95) 284-0616. A magnificent and atmospheric restaurant built inside the bullring. Creative fish and vegetable cooking. Try **rabo de toro**; it is the house speciality.

TOURS AND EXCURSIONS

Local travel agencies and coach companies operate tours all over the coast and interior, most with a pick up point in Málaga city. Coastal destinations include **Nerja**, **Mijas**, **Marbella** and **Gibraltar**, while longer day trips operate to **Granada**, **Sevilla**, **Córdoba**, **Ronda** and **Tangier**. Any travel agent will book places on an excursion. All trips are operated in air-conditioned buses with an English-speaking guide and all tours cost approximately the same.

El Chorro and **El Torcal** have to be explored independently, as they are off the beaten tourist trail. The El Torcal ranger will supply free maps and details of marked walks.

USEFUL CONTACTS

A useful tip is to collect as much information as possible about Spain from your local Spanish Tourist Board. Even the most basic maps and brochures incur a charge in Spain and calling at the tourist board in every town can add alarmingly to the cost of your trip.

Tourist Information Office, Pasaje de Chinitas 4, Málaga, tel: (95) 221-3445. Provides brochures and maps at a nominal charge and the excellent guide called *Hiking in Andalucía*.

Municipal Tourist Office, Plaza Guerrero Munoz S/N, Antequera, tel: (95) 270-4051.

Agencie de Medio Ambiente, Calle Molina Larios 13, 29015 Málaga, tel: (95) 222-5800, fax: (95) 222-5807. Environmental agency issuing permits to visit protected areas.

MALAGA	J	F	M	A	M	J	J	A	S	O	N	D
AVERAGE TEMP. °C	13	13	15	16	19	23	24	25	23	20	17	13
AVERAGE TEMP. °F	55	55	59	61	66	73	75	77	73	68	63	55
HOURS OF SUN DAILY	6	6	6	8	10	11	11	11	9	7	6	5
RAINFALL mm	150	150	150	200	125	–	–	–	75	125	150	175
RAINFALL in	6	6	6	8	5	–	–	–	3	5	6	7
DAYS OF RAINFALL	7	6	6	6	3	–	–	–	5	6	6	7

3
West of Málaga

Stretching due west of Málaga is most people's vision of the 'typical' Costa del Sol. **Torremolinos** and **Fuengirola** were two of the original fishing villages earmarked for development in the 1960s and today are big, brash, urban sprawls of tower blocks and neon lights along wide, sandy beaches with row after row of sun umbrellas covering legions of basking sun-worshippers. Today, there's hardly a fishing fleet in sight.

The **N340,** the main highway linking the string of holiday resorts basking on this stretch of coast, actually follows the route of an ancient Roman road that was built to link the city of Cádiz to Rome. This fast, dual carriageway snakes around the towns, occasionally cut right into the mountainside, with tantalizing glimpses of the cool, blue Mediterranean Sea.

Beyond Fuengirola, the tower blocks become *urbanizaciones*, sprawling estates of low-rise, Moorish-style houses in dazzling white. Dense pine forests form a scented canopy and private homes begin to resemble little turreted palaces against a backdrop of the high mountains. West of **Marbella**, easily the most glamorous resort on the coast, lies the **Golden Mile**, where wealthy homes lie on luxuriant, sub-tropical estates.

Whatever the various charms of each resort, visitors in search of the 'real' Spain will have to head inland to find anything remotely Andalucían. Just a short distance will suffice, to the sleepy hill villages of **Benalmádena**, **Mijas** and **Ojén**, where the air is much cooler and the Mediterranean becomes a blue blur in the heat haze.

MEDITERRANEAN SEA

DON'T MISS

*** Marbella: wander round a typically Andalucían district.
*** Fuengirola: has the best flea market on the coast.
** Mijas: watch a stunning sunset from the village.
** Torremolinos: barbecued sardines on skewers over a fire on the beach.
** Benalmádena Pueblo and **Coín:** explore the wonderfully unspoilt villages.
** Puerto Banús: the glamorous place to people-watch.
* Nueva Andalucía: for a round of golf on one the immaculate courses.

Opposite: *The best way to arrive in glamorous Puerto Banús is by boat.*

TORREMOLINOS

Big, brash, colourful and loud, Torremolinos, the first resort west of Málaga airport, is a resort for the young and lively, with two vast expanses of beach dedicated to sun-worshipping and neon-lit streets that throng with life.

Torre de los Molinos, the tower of the windmills, is recorded on a map as early as 1748, when the village was surrounded by 19 flour mills, powered by three streams flowing into the Mediterranean at El Bajondillo beach. The 'torre' itself is an even earlier Moorish watchtower and can still be seen at the end of **Calle San Miguel**.

Calle San Miguel today is a riot of bars, pubs, amusement arcades and souvenir shops and leads to a flight of steps descending to the beaches of **La Carihuela** and **Bajondillo**, divided by a rocky promontory. La Carihuela, the original fishing village that used to serve Málaga, still bears traces of its humble past and ancient fishermen can be spotted here in the morning, grilling wooden skewers of silvery sardines over open fires on the beach.

Despite its largely transient population, Torremolinos has some 30,000 permanent inhabitants who turn out in style each September for a spectacular *romería* in honour of **San Miguel**, the town's patron saint. A colourful parade of ox-drawn gypsy caravans, beautiful Andalucían horses and flamenco dancers weaves through the streets to the pine forest behind the town for a night of barbecues, *paella* cooking, *fino* drinking and dancing.

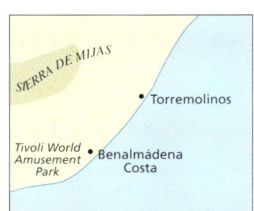

BENALMADENA

Somewhat tamer than its neighbour, Benalmádena forms three separate areas: the big strip of hotels along the coast and around the new *puerto*; the **Arroyo de la Miel**, a lively suburb packed with bars, restaurants and shops; and **Benalmádena Pueblo**, the original village set back from the coast in the hills.

Approximately 20,000 people inhabit this area and **Benalmádena** is filled with life throughout the year. In summer, the village provides a cool refuge from the hectic pace of the coast, its steep, narrow alleys leading to tiny squares, balconies bursting with geraniums. The main square, **Plaza de España**, contains the statue that has become the emblem of Benalmádena – a young girl offering water in an upturned shell. A small municipal museum contains artefacts from the bronze and middle ages which have been found locally. There's a magnificent view of the coast from the tiny church at the top of the village, including a somewhat incongruous fairytale castle below, a folly built by a wealthy Spanish doctor.

Along the shoreline are three reminders of Benalmádena's Phoenician inhabitants – stone watchtowers, built to look out for pirate invaders. The **Castillo de Bil-Bil**, an unlikely-looking castle on the seafront is not a monument, but a former private house built in the 1980s and recently converted into an exhibition hall.

Benalmádena's new port, fast becoming one of the most chic along the coast with its restaurants, shops and cocktail bars, is lively at night and has a small aquarium to visit. Children will also enjoy **Tivoli World** in the Arroyo, a permanent amusement park with gardens, fountains, restaurants and bars as well as rides, open from 16:00 to midnight.

Below: *The lights of Torremolinos are the brightest of the Costa del Sol.*

FUENGIROLA

Heading west, Fuengirola is the next big resort, situated about 9km (6 miles) along the coast from Benalmádena Costa and the most family orientated of the three. Its main attraction is a big, safe sweep of beach. Various theme parks are planned, and the whole seafront was remodelled in 1999.

In the old part of the town, bars and restaurants are clustered around the **Plaza de la Constitución**, which is lively in the evenings. Much of the resort, however, is modern and built up, a Moorish castle, **Castillo de Sohail**, surveying the tower blocks from its hill. Flattened on command of the Catholic kings, the castle was rebuilt in the 18th century and occupied by French troops in the Peninsular War in 1808, reminders of which can be seen in the cannons guarding the **Paseo Maritimo**. Recently restored, the castle can be explored on foot.

Children will love the **Parque Aquatico** in Fuengirola, just outside the town on the Mijas road. Water slides and tubes keep older children amused, while a separate mini-park caters for toddlers. The park is open daily from 10:30–17:30 (May), 10:00–18:00 (June and September), 10:00–19:00 (July–August), and under fours get in free.

MIJAS ★★★

Perched among pine forests on a mountainside just 8km (5 miles) inland from the urban sprawl of Fuengirola, the pretty village of Mijas is besieged by day-trippers in search of a typical Andalucían *pueblo*. The village is unquestionably attractive but its biggest irony is that foreign residents outnumber Spaniards by a long way.

Like many Andalucían villages, Mijas has **Roman**, **Phoenician** and **Moorish** origins and its present layout dates back to Moorish times, with a tiny section of the fortifying wall visible near the parish church, formerly the site of a mosque. The village served as a **granary** for Fuengirola, a defence stronghold against the Christians (until the surrender of Málaga, when the villagers gave in), and in the 17th and 18th centuries as housing for the workers of the now disused agate and marble quarries in the hills. The stone from the quarries was used in Málaga's Cathedral and the Alcazaba in Sevilla.

Just before sunset is the best time to visit, when the coach parties have headed back down the mountain road, the light is golden and the craft and curio shops are still open. Mijas is small enough to explore on foot, although *burro* (donkey) 'taxis' and carriages wait patiently by the car park to ferry visitors through the narrow streets.

SIERRA DE MIJAS

Mijas •

Torreblanca
del Sol •

• Fuengirola

CHILDREN ON THE COSTA DEL SOL

The Spanish love children and restaurants are happy to serve families late into the evening, a common occurrence here. There is a growing number of attractions for children along the coast. Try the **aquarium** at Benalmádena Puerto and the **aquapark** at Mijas, which has waterslides and tubes, suitable for all ages. **Tivoli World** at Benalmádena is a permanent funfair, open year round and older children will enjoy the bird of prey centre near Marbella. Travel agents can also book **donkey safaris** around the mountain village of Coín; the donkeys trek to an old farmhouse where games with prizes take place and *paella* is served.

Opposite: *The Aquapark at Mijas makes a great day out for children.*
Left: *Foreign residents outnumber Spaniards in the pretty mountain village of Mijas.*

Above: *The bullring at Mijas is unusual in that it is square.*

There are several things to see. From the sanctuary of the **Virgen de la Pena**, the patron saint of the village, there are spectacular views of the coast, sprinkled with luxury villas, azure pools and golf courses, the tower blocks of Fuengirola hazy in the distance. Inside the shrine is a carved **wooden statue** of the virgin dating back to AD850.

Mijas has a square **bullring**, built in 1920, located just in front of the parish church which is built on the site of an Arabic mosque. There's also a colourful **bullfighting museum** showing interesting scenes of the great matadors and taurean memorabilia.

The narrow streets are crammed with craft and souvenir shops selling everything from carved wooden bowls to lace shawls, ceramics and the inevitable T-shirts. A couple of small art galleries are worth a browse and the town hall has a display of the work of local artists, as well as some farming tools and artefacts from former generations. A new folk museum was opened opposite the post office in 1995.

High above the village is the **Calvario Hermitage**, a tiny chapel built around 1710. Black iron crosses mark a short walking trail through the pine forest, with sweeping views of the coast and the village below as a reward.

MARBELLA

Marbella enjoyed its heyday as a haunt of the rich and famous in the 1970s, when tourism to the Costa del Sol was booming and famous names lined the guest lists of super-deluxe and super-discreet hotels like **Los Monteros**, **Puente Romano** and the **Marbella Club**.

While the glamour is less obvious nowadays, Marbella continues to be a pleasant and often overlooked way to spend half a day. Much of the interest for tourists is in the **casco antiguo**, the old town, the focal point of which is the **Plaza de los Naranjos**, or orange tree square, dating back to 1485. Despite the sun umbrellas packing the centre, the wrought iron, geranium-filled balconies and intriguing little streets going off at every angle give the square a wonderful atmosphere of another age. Each alleyway is lined with shops and restaurants to tempt the pocket and the taste buds. The white, Moorish houses are beautifully preserved, with every street name and house number in colourful ceramic tiles.

ARABIC INFLUENCE

An estimated 10 to 15% of Spanish words have Arabic origins and place names in Andalucía, in particular, date back to Moorish times. **Guad**, for example, means river, hence Guadalquivir, Guadalhorce, Guadalmina. **Al-mariya** (Almería) means 'mirror of the sea', while **Jebel al-Tariq** (Gibraltar) means 'the mountain of Tariq', after the first Moorish general that landed on the Iberian peninsula.
   Al-Djezirah al Hadra (Algeciras) means 'Green Island'. **Mulhacen**, the highest peak in the Sierra Nevada, is named after the father of **Boabdil**, Granada's last Moorish king.

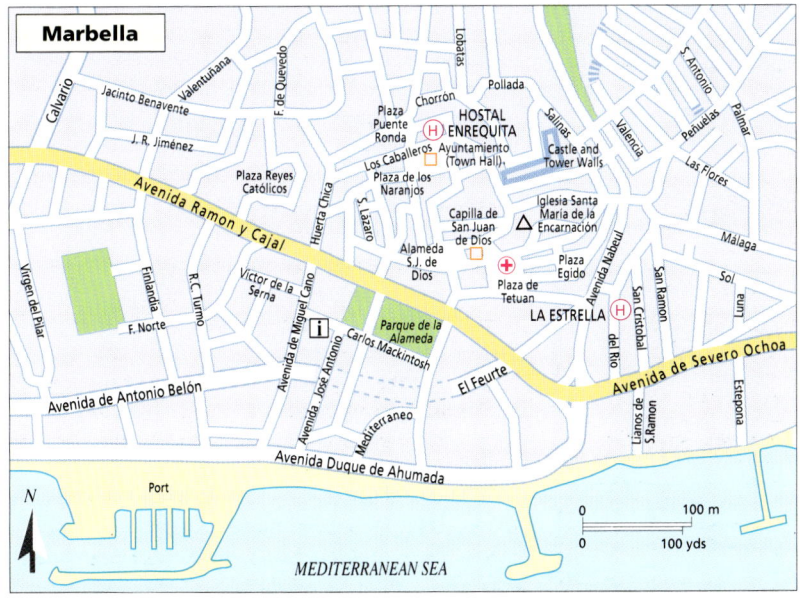

Above: *Marbella's Plaza de los Narajos is a popular meeting place to enjoy a cup of morning coffee.*

THE N340

The Costa del Sol's main highway, the N340, is notorious for accidents and should be treated with extreme caution. While the 'N' signifies a principal carriageway, the road passes through all the coastal resorts, so always be on the lookout for traffic lights and at night beware of inebriated tourists dashing across the four lanes. Never make illegal left turns – use the *cambio de sentido* turn-offs to change directions.

On **Plaza de los Naranjos** is the lovely **Ayuntamiento** (town hall), a graceful 1568 building, with a stone inscription commemorating the reconquest of the town by Los Reyes Católicos in 1485. Next door is the tourist office, formerly the house of the chief justice, with a façade dating back to 1602. The fountain on the opposite side was placed in the square in 1504 by the first Christian mayor of the town.

Head out of the square at the top right-hand corner and look at the crumbling city walls, interspersed with the yellow and white painted houses. The southern alleyway from the square leads to the **Santa María** church, surprisingly large in this maze of tiny alleys. Inside, the modern organ, built in 1972, is made of 5000 pewter, copper and wooden pipes.

A morning exploring the shops, most of them decidedly upmarket, and stopping in the **Plaza de los Naranjos** for freshly squeezed juice, Italian ice cream or a *café con leche* (coffee with hot milk), passes quickly. Marbella's real designer alley, however, is the **Avenida Ramon y Cajal**, which forms the southern border of the casco antiguo, a palm-lined boulevard of everything from Gucci to Benetton. Cross over to the **Alameda**, a tiny, tree-filled park where locals sit and gossip on brilliantly coloured ceramic benches under banana palms, in the cooling mist of a fountain. A marble walkway leads from here to the beach, although the three smartest hotels and the best beach clubs are located just out of town.

For the botanical enthusiast, Marbella also has a small **Bonsai Museum** (open 10:00–13:30, 16:00–19:00 in winter; 10:00–13:30, 17:00–20:00 in summer), a lovingly tended collection of miniature trees, cultivated in the Japanese style to be perfect, dwarf versions of the real thing. A 300-year-old olive tree and some *pinsapo* firs are the museum's prize specimens, nestling among rocks taken from the **El Torcal National Park**.

Also worth noting is the vast mosque, next to which is one of the palaces of former King Fahd of Saudi Arabia, a replica of the White House and just visible from the turn-off to the Marbella Club.

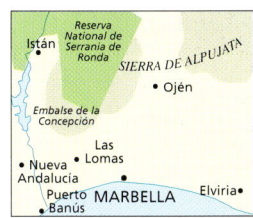

Nueva Andalucía

A chic suburb of Marbella, Nueva Andalucía sprawls across the hills behind the town, elegant estates of luxury villas overlooking three exclusive golf courses: **Aloha Golf**, **Las Brisas** and **Los Naranjos**. Many of the residents are former inhabitants of Marbella who have retreated to the hills in search of privacy.

Nueva Andalucía's most famous attraction is **Puerto Banús**, one of Spain's first village-style port developments. Whitewashed condominiums are grouped around a large marina filled with the most luxurious yachts imaginable, while Rolls-Royces and Ferraris cruise slowly past outdoor restaurants and cafés. The people are undeniably colourful and sitting at one of the bars watching the world go by is a popular pastime on a summer evening. Puerto Banús has not escaped the advance of mass tourism, however, and souvenir shops and a huge cinema complex are intermingled with designer boutiques. The port is currently being extended to accommodate transatlantic cruise liners, which will bring more crowds into the area.

Left: *Puerto Banús was one of Spain's first village-style port developments.*

BALLOONING

Marbella-based **Aviación del Sol**, tel: (95) 287-7249, arranges hot air balloon trips over the coast and mountains. An evening flight over Marbella and the surrounding resorts is followed by champagne and *tapas* on landing. The views across the Strait of Gibraltar at sunset are breathtaking, while a pre-drawn trip over the stunning Ronda mountains and the White Towns is finished in style with champagne breakfast.

OJÉN

High in the hills behind the coast is the tiny village of Ojén, 19km (12 miles) off the N340 outside Marbella. Set among eucalyptus and citrus groves, this whitewashed *pueblo* is a typical example of an Andalucían village. The area used to be famous for iron and steel manufacture, but Ojén earned its place on the map through the manufacture of an *anise* drink called **Aguardiente**, now languishing in the gastronomic history books. This *eau de vie* was believed to be beneficial to the respiratory system. The name occasionally appears on bottles elsewhere in Spain.

North of the village, a tiny track turns off the main road into the **Reserva Nacional de Serranía de Ronda**, a hunting reserve belonging to the Ronda district. Here, the **Refúgio de Juanar**, a pretty country house with roaring log fires in winter, nestles above chestnuts and *pinsapo* trees on the site of an old hunting lodge belonging to an aristocratic Spanish family. The house is now run by the villagers of Ojén and its excellent restaurant specializes in game that would not be found on the coast; marinated partridge, rabbit, venison, quail and even mountain goat.

Walking trails are marked all around the Refúgio through the *pinsapo* forest. A gentle 2.5km (2 miles) hike up the hill to 1000m (3281ft) above sea level, a *mirador* (viewing point) looks out over the coast and, on a clear day, as far as Africa. Wildlife is abundant in the forest and includes golden eagle, eagle owl, hare and the rare Spanish ibex, a mountain goat that lives on the rocky upper slopes. Keen hikers can follow trails back towards Ojén or west to the village of Istán.

Below: *Colours change constantly on the exposed, upper slopes of the Serranía de Ronda.*

TOP ATTRACTIONS
Markets

Markets move up and down the Costa del Sol all week and are guaranteed to produce bargains as well as plenty of local colour. *'Barato'* is the general term for market while a *'rastro'* is a flea market, the best of which takes place on Saturday morning (09:00–14:00) around the bullring in **Nueva Andalucía**. Leather from Morocco, ceramics, lace, antiques, woodcarvings, hats, T-shirts and jewellery are all on sale. For more of an emphasis on arts and crafts, **Puerto Sotogrande** has a market on Sunday mornings.

Typical products of Spain on sale in all the main resorts include **ceramics**, **leather goods**, many of them from the Whites Towns around Ronda; **pearls** from Mallorca and **Lladró** figurines, sold all over the world. **Ceramics** shops are everywhere and the standard varies from very basic unglazed pots to exquisite pieces from the **Cartuja de Sevilla** factory. **Woven rugs** and **baskets** are also a good buy, although there is more choice in their villages of origin, around Ronda and in the Alpujarras south of Granada.

Traditional items like **castanets**, **shawls**, **flamenco dresses** and decorative **combs** may look like clichés but you only have to attend a festival and see Spanish women in their finery to realize that these are essential to the local culture. Buy these items in local shops, not souvenir stalls.

Above: *Ceramics are a good buy; look out for 'ceramica' signs along the main roads.*

Above: *Golfers are spoilt for choice with over 40 courses and more opening all the time.*

Golf

Golfers will think they are in heaven on the Costa del Sol with a staggering 40 courses packed into the 120km (75 miles) stretch of coast between Málaga and La Línea, the border town between Spain and the tiny British colony of Gibraltar.

Some of the world's best courses are here including **Valderrama** – one of the finest – designed by **Robert Trent Jones** and the setting of the 1997 **Ryder Cup**. Famous golfing names are everywhere; **Tony Jacklin** is director of the **San Roque** club and Spanish Ryder Cup hero **Seve Ballesteros** runs **Los Arqueros**, in the hills near the village of Benahavis.

All types of terrain are waiting to be explored, from sweeping fairways between cork oaks and pine woods on the Sotogrande course to the wind-blown links of Alcaidesa at La Línea and the hilly, hazard-packed **La Duquesa**, owned by **José María Canizares**, former member of the European Ryder Cup team.

Generally speaking, the courses get more upmarket and expensive west of Marbella, where the rolling hills and millionaires' villas of Nueva Andalucía overlook three very ritzy clubs; **Aloha Golf**, **Las Brisas** and **Los Naranjos**. There is one municipal course, **La Cañada**, just before San Roque, and some clubs, including the friendly **Golf El Paraiso** club at Estepona and the **Miraflores** club at Mijas Costa are genuinely welcoming to visitors. Otherwise, almost all courses demand a handicap certificate and in the high golfing season, January to May and September to November, it is essential to book tee-times well in advance to secure a game.

Sporting Holidays

Many people use a visit to the Costa del Sol as an opportunity to learn a new sport, or improve an existing one. **Golf lessons** are available at most courses, although there are a couple of specialist golf schools, the Escuela de Golf La Quinta at Marbella, directed by three times world champion Manuel Piñero and the Atalaya Golf School in Estepona, which runs courses in technique improvement. Benalmádena has a **scuba diving** school operating out of Puerto Marina, taking beginners to a level of proficiency sufficient for open water dives. Just inland, on Medrana lake, signposted from the Ronda road, is one of only 70 **cable ski** centres worldwide. This is an ideal way to learn to waterski, with no wake and no waves to contend with. Skiers are towed along by a rope attached to a wire that crosses the lake.

On dry land, the Campo de Tennis run by former Wimbledon champion Lew Hoad arranges **tennis** courses and tournaments throughout the year, while Spanish star Manolo Santana, also a Wimbledon champion, runs an exclusive tennis club at the Puente Romano hotel. **Riding** lessons, meanwhile, take place at the Los Monteros Hotel riding school and the Lakeview Equestrian Centre at San Pedro.

> **MARINAS ON THE COSTA DEL SOL**
>
> Following the huge popularity of **Puerto Banús**, Spain's first '*pueblo*' port, many picturesque marinas have sprung up all along the Costa del Sol. Signposted '*puerto deportivo*', most are pretty yacht harbours with shops and restaurants overlooking the moorings. Recommended marinas to visit for a stroll and a drink are **Marina del Este** in Granada province in a lovely setting at the foot of a cliff; **Benalmádena Puerto**, one of the newest, with lively nightlife; **Puerto Cabopino**, just outside Marbella; and La **Duquesa** towards Gibraltar, a smaller version of Puerto Banús. **Sotogrande** also has a very smart marina.

Below: *Tennis fans will find plenty of opportunities for a game.*

West of Málaga at a Glance

BEST TIMES TO VISIT

Summer is the liveliest time and the height of the tourist season. **Winters** are mild and pleasant and most attractions are open, although places like Puerto Banús will not be so busy out of season.

GETTING THERE

This area of the coast is easily accessible by road from **Málaga International Airport**. Torremolinos is about 20 minutes' drive, while Marbella is one hour maximum. Málaga is served by **international flights** from major European cities and **domestic flights** from Spanish cities. Gibraltar is also a gateway airport, about one hour and 20 minutes from Marbella, served daily by **GB Airways** from London.

GETTING AROUND

The **Portillo** bus company runs a comprehensive service up and down the coast and to the villages of Benalmádena Pueblo and Mijas. **Information** from **tourist offices** or the **bus station** in Marbella, tel: (95) 277-2192. Car rental is available in all the main resorts and at **Málaga Airport**.

WHERE TO STAY

LUXURY
Marbella Club, Bulevard Principe Alfonso de Hohenlohe, S/N, tel: (95) 282-2211, fax: (95) 282-9884.

Andalucían and Moroccan style in beautiful gardens on Marbella's Golden Mile.
Hotel Puente Romano, Ctra. Nac. 340, km178, 29600 Marbella, tel: (95) 277-0100, fax: (95) 277-5766. Jetset resort hotel next to the Marbella Club.
Hotel Byblos Andaluz, Urbanizacion Mijas Golf, 29650 Mijas, Málaga, tel: (95) 246-0250, fax: (95) 247-6783. Deluxe hotel with a superb health spa and award-winning restaurant in the hills just below Mijas.

MID-RANGE
La Fonda de Benalmádena, c/Santo Domingo 7, Benalmádena Pueblo, 29639 Málaga, tel: and fax: (95) 256-8273. Pretty, 26-room Andalucían-style hotel in Benalmádena village.
Refúgio de Juanar, Sierra Blanca, 29610 Ojén, Málaga, tel: and fax: (95) 288-1001. Mountainside lodge in nature reserve behind Marbella, specializes in game food.
Hotel Mijas, Urb. Tamisa S/N, 29650 Mijas (Málaga), tel: (95) 248-5800, fax: (95) 248-5825. Comfortable three-star hotel with beautiful views, located just outside Mijas.

BUDGET
Hostal Enrequita, 29600 Marbella (Málaga), tel: (95) 282-7552. Two-star town house close to Marbella's old quarter.

Hotel Miami, Aladino 14, 29620 Torremolinos, Málaga, tel: (95) 238-5255. Hotel built around old mansion house in Carihuela district.

WHERE TO EAT

Main concentrations of restaurants are in Marbella's *casco antiguo*; Puerto Banús; La Carihuela section of Torremolinos; Benalmádena Puerto and Arroyo de la Miel and in Fuengirola centre. While Puerto Banús is good for people-watching, most restaurants there are over-priced and overrated.

Marbella
La Meridiana, Camino de la Cruz, Marbella, tel: (95) 277-6190. Rated by Spanish *Gourmet* magazine as one of the best. Closed lunchtime.
El Portalón, Carretera de Cádiz km178, Marbella, tel: (95) 282-7880, fax: (95) 286-1075. High quality, traditional cooking on Golden Mile.
Albahaca, Calle Lobatas 31, Marbella, tel: (952) 286-3520. Largely vegetarian restaurant specializing in Andalucían and Galician dishes.
Marisqueria La Pesquería, Plaza de la Victoria, 29600 Marbella, tel: (952) 277-8054. Fish restaurant in the old town serving excellent *tapas*.
Dalli's Pasta Factory, Puerto Banús, tel: (95) 281-2490. Popular pasta restaurant run by local chain, representing good value in Puerto Banús.

West of Málaga at a Glance

Torremolinos

La Carihuela, the old fishing village, is lined with lively restaurants. Cuisine ranging from British to Italian, Swedish and Indian available in the town centre.

Casa Juan, La Carihuela, tel: (95) 237-6523. Famous fish restaurant, great atmosphere and reasonable prices.

El Comedor, Calle Casablanca S/N, Torremolinos, tel: (95) 238-2881. Basque specialities including mouthwatering seafood crêpes and venison.

Benalmádena

Hotel Torrequebrada, Café Royal, Casino Torrequebrada, 29630 Benalmádena Costa, tel: (95) 244-6000. Big casino complex with gourmet restaurant, gaming rooms and La Fortuna flamenco show.

Fuengirola

La Casa Vieja, Avenida de las Boliches 27, Las Boliches, tel: (95) 258-3830. Village house with patio serving Spanish specialities.

SHOPPING

Marbella's main shopping street is **Avenida Ramon y Cajal**, lined with boutiques and designer stores. Arts and crafts stores are around the **Plaza de los Naranjos** and there's a good flea market at the bullring of **Nueva Andalucía** on Saturdays. Puerto Banús is lined with designer shops and souvenir stalls. Mijas

and Benalmádena Pueblo villages have interesting arts and crafts shops and there's a huge market on Tuesdays and Sundays at Fuengirola village.

TOURS AND EXCURSIONS

Sava Travel, Avda. Bonanza S/N, Benalmádena (Málaga), tel: (95) 244-4712. Guided tours to Ronda, Granada, Gibraltar and Sevilla, with pick-ups in each resort.

Yasmine Line Travel, Avda. Alay Local 27, Benalmádena Costa, tel: (95) 244-5576, fax: (95) 256-1627. Regular excursions to Tangier and Gibraltar from Benalmádena.

Marbella

Escuela de Golf La Quinta, tel: (95) 278-3462, fax: (95) 278-3466. Golf tuition at all levels at school founded by three times world champion Manuel Pinero.

Mountain Bike Aventura, Pueblo Platero 8, Bloque 1, Elviria, Las Chapas, Marbella, tel: (952) 283-1204. Mountain bike hire and guided tours in rural areas close to coast.

The Riding School, Hotel Los Monteros, Urb. Rio Real, Ctra. Cádiz km185, tel: (95) 277-1700. Lessons and hacks from the Los Monteros Hotel.

Torremolinos

Pepe Lopez, Plaza de la Bamba Alegre, Torremolinos, tel: (95) 238-1284. Reasonably authentic and enjoyable flamenco *tablao*.

Autos Lara Jeep Safari, Calle Salvador Allende S/N, Torremolinos, tel: (95) 138-1800, fax: (95) 238-1081. Full day jeep tours daily to El Chorro and Ardales National Park.

Benalmádena

Campo de Tenis de Lew Hadd's, Ctra. de Mijas km3.5, Mijas, tel: (95) 247-4858. Tennis club run by the former champion Lew Hoad. Lessons, clinics, informal games and tournaments.

El Ranchito, Benalmádena, tel: (95) 238-3140. Lesser, unrelated version of the Jerez School of Equestrian Art with dressage and horsemanship displays.

Castillo de Aguilas, Benalmádena Pueblo, tel: (95) 256-8484. Birds of prey centre; eagles, falcons and variety of indigenuos birds are fed daily.

Tivoli World, Arroyo de la Miel, Benalmádena, tel: (95) 244-5044. Big funfair with rides, shows, exhibitions and extensive gardens.

Diving Centre, Club Nautico, tel: (95) 256-0769.

USEFUL CONTACTS

Municipal Tourist Offices:
Marbella, Glorieta de la Fontanilla, tel: (95) 277-1442.
Benalmádena Costa, Ctra. de Cádiz km220, tel: (95) 244-2494, website: www.pta.es/benalmadena
Torremolinos, Plaza blas Infante 1, tel: (95) 238-1578, fax: (95) 237-9551.

4
Western
Costa del Sol

The western end of the Costa del Sol becomes less developed beyond Marbella, the hillsides sprinkled with stark white *urbanizaciones* and well-tended golf courses either side of the only major resort, **Estepona**. The area is nonetheless rich in history and culture with some interesting **Roman remains** outside San Pedro de Alcántara, the daily **fish auction** in Estepona, the beautiful white village of **Casares** and attractive new **port** developments at Estepona, Sotogrande and Duquesa.

Wide beaches with rolling surf line the coast, with pine forests and cork oak woods covering gentle hills behind **Sotogrande** – a resort and golf complex at the far western end of the coast. The **Rock of Gibraltar** looms in the distance and beyond, the purple, hazy mountains of **Morocco** are visible across the Strait of Gibraltar. The Rock, or 'Gib', as the locals call it, is packed with military history and as a British colony and offshore financial centre, enjoys duty-free status and attracts a lot of shoppers.

Visitors taking day trips to **Tangier** for shopping of a different kind in the bustling Moroccan *souks* will bypass Gibraltar for the busy port of **Algeciras** from which ferries and hydrofoils depart for North Africa. Beyond Algeciras on the southern tip of Spain, windsurfers flock to **Tarifa**, wind and wave capital of Europe.

SAN PEDRO DE ALCANTARA
Unlike the big holiday resorts, San Pedro de Alcántara, immediately west of Marbella and Estepona, some 20km (12½ miles) further on, are genuine 'Spanish' communities

DON'T MISS

*** **Gibraltar:** a day in the historic British colony.
*** **Tangier:** browsing for bargains in the *souks*.
** **Sotogrande:** horse riding at sunset along the beach.
** **Tarifa:** Europe's most exciting windsurfing.
* **Puerto Duquesa:** have dinner in this fashionable '*pueblo*' port.

Opposite: *An atalaya, an ancient watchtower, is silhouetted in the sunrise over Estepona.*

with a relaxed, easy-going lifestyle. There are plenty of hidden squares where locals sip coffee or an early *fino* and read the daily newspapers in the morning sun.

Villa Romana de Río Verde *

On the beach side of the road between Puerto Banús and San Pedro (leave the main road before the Puente Romano Hotel and follow the signs) are the remains of a first-century **Roman villa** in which unusual black and white mosaic flooring has been remarkably well preserved. The mosaics are surprising in that they depict culinary objects – cooking pots, jugs, water pitchers and cooking utensils, as well as birds, fish and a Medusa's head. The villa was discovered in 1962 and is believed to have had three corridors and a patio surrounded by five rooms. For opening times, enquire at the tourist office on Plaza de la Iglesia.

Basílica de Vega del Mar *

Situated on the right-hand side of the main road leading from San Pedro to the beach are the foundations of an important **Visigothic Christian basilica**, dating back to the sixth century. The basilica, surrounded by a graveyard, was discovered in the tenth century as eucalyptus forests were being planted along the coast. Some of the riches retrieved from the graves are in the Museum of Archaeology in Madrid. Note the baptismal font, which is over 1m (3ft) deep – the Visigothic Christians baptized both children and adults by total immersion.

Las Bovedas *

Just along the beach from the basilica is the shell of a **Roman bathhouse**, discovered in 1926. The seven chambers, serving as steam rooms in the third century, are constructed around an octagonal patio above a central, octagonal bath. A circular gallery on the upper floors gives access to several smaller rooms. While the evidence for this being a bathhouse seems solid, there is a theory that the structure was an enclosed reservoir for water carried by the nearby aqueducts.

ESTEPONA

A pleasant town 26km (16 miles) west of Marbella, with a long seafront promenade overlooking a wide, sandy beach, Estepona's focal point is the **Plaza de las Flores**, a pretty square lined with cafés off the **Calle Santa Ana**. Remnants of old castle walls and whitewashed buildings with red tiled roofs and geranium-filled balconies in the narrow streets of the old town are the only reminder of the Moorish era that ended 500 years ago.

Estepona supports a large fishing fleet and in the *puerto* coloured fishing boats line up alongside luxury yachts. A lively fish auction takes place every morning, although it's over by 07:00. The covered market on **Calle Castillo** is also worth a visit for the wide range of fresh fruit and vegetables and, of course, fish.

SOTOGRANDE

Sotogrande, a wealthy estate and marina complex with condominiums, restaurants and hotels is unusual in that it is the heart of the Spanish polo scene.

Many visitors come to play golf on the estate's four exclusive courses including **Valderrama**, home of the 1997 Ryder Cup, but a new wave of tourist is being attracted by the prospect of Spain's only permanent **polo** field. Visitors can enjoy polo society reminiscent of Deauville or Palm Beach, with regular matches in July, August and September and practice matches throughout June.

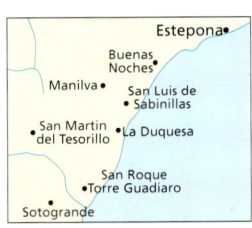

POLO

Polo originated in **Persia** where it was played in a rather macabre fashion with the corpse of a goat. The game spread throughout **Turkey** and **Tibet** to **India**, where British army officers learnt to play, this time with a ball. They soon spread the word to the west and polo developed as a rather upmarket pastime, requiring extensive funds to support the necessary string of highly trained ponies.

The warm climate and extensive stabling of **Sotogrande** have been a magnet to polo players since the mid-1980s, British and Argentinian teams training here during their respective winters. Now, for an unusual kind of holiday, complete beginners can try their hand and be practising chukkas within a week.

Opposite: *One of the many ruined watchtowers that once guarded the Costa del Sol.*
Left: *Estepona's fish auction is worth a visit – if you can get up at dawn.*

WATER CATCHMENT

At the beginning of this century, massive water catchment slopes were constructed on the eastern side of Gibraltar, covering 34ha (84 acres) of a 100,000-year-old sand dune. Rainfall was conveyed by channels into reservoirs inside the Rock holding 16 million gallons of water. Gibraltar now gets its water from desalinization plants but the water catchment slopes remain a feature of the landscape.

GIBRALTAR

A massive chunk of ancient limestone thrust up from the sea beds and flipped on its back some 200 million years ago, Gibraltar is visible from miles around, forming a tiny peninsula between the Spanish town of **La Línea** on the Costa del Sol and the industrial city of **Algeciras**. Just 6km (4 miles) long, 2km (1¼ miles) wide and a towering 450m (1476ft) high, Gibraltar has been the scene of one military tussle after another because of its important strategic location, guarding the entrance to the Mediterranean, just 13km (8 miles) from the coast of Africa. The narrow strait is the only outlet through which Mediterranean water can flow into the Atlantic Ocean.

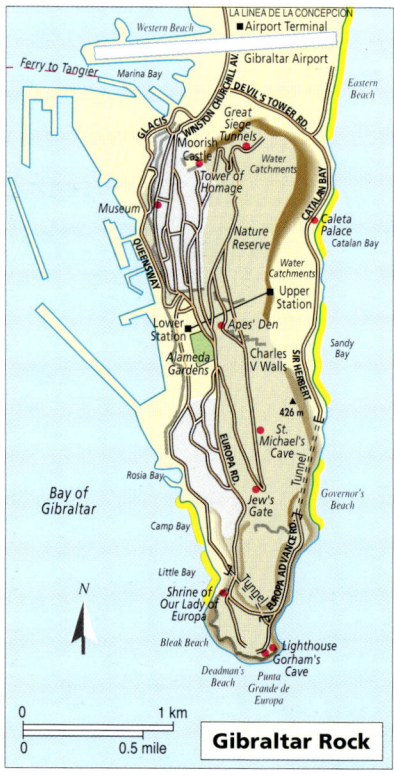

The rock is riddled with caves and passageways, many of which have yet to be explored. Human bones dating back 120,000 years have been found here. Gibraltar's first important role in military history, however, was in AD711, when Tariq ibn-Ziyad, governor of Tangier, landed here with a huge Moorish army and embarked on his conquest of southern Spain. For 600 years, **Jebel-al-Tariq** (the rock of Tariq) as it was then known, formed part of the Moorish kingdom of al-Andalus. Between 1309 and 1462 the Spanish Christians made several attempts to claim the rock, finally succeeding and sending the Moors back to Africa. A joint Anglo–Dutch army took Gibraltar in 1704 and after several desperate attempts to win it back, culminating in the Great Siege of 1779, the Spanish gave up. To this day, Gibraltar has remained a British colony and an important naval base, although the question of its sovereignty occasionally arises. General Franco closed the border with Spain in 1967 and it only reopened in 1985.

Left: *Gibraltar's dramatic cliffs can be seen for miles.*

Touring the Rock

Official guides can be booked through the tourist office for the 90-minute tour of Gibraltar, although independent exploration on foot is possible. Do not try to take a car across the border as parking is difficult.

Upper Rock Nature Reserve ★★★

Accessible by road or the cable car (open daily 9:30–19:00) which leaves from the Alameda Gardens on Main Street, the Upper Rock area contains some 600 species of plants, some of them unique to Gibraltar. Several attractions are located within the reserve.

Great Siege Tunnels ★★★

These galleries were dug in 1779 and are regarded as a spectacular piece of engineering, allowing the British forces to position their guns at extraordinary heights, an advantage which won the Great Siege. There are around 48km (30 miles) of tunnels now, most of them closed to the public, although wax dummies depict scenes of hardship, showing British soldiers digging into the rock.

ROCK MYTHOLOGY

The Romans believed Gibraltar to be one of the two Pillars of Hercules; the second, Jebel Musa, is visible across the Strait. The geological reality is somewhat different – movement of the continental plates caused a fissure to open about five million years ago, separating what are now Europe and Africa, and water gushed in from the Atlantic over a 3048m (10,000ft) waterfall, taking 100 years to fill the barren Mediterranean basin. Because the narrow channel causes violent winds and storms to blow up, and because the Bay of Gibraltar is so deep at over 800m (2625ft), sailors have always had a healthy respect for the seas round Gibraltar without the need for superstition.

Opposite: *Each of the Barbary apes on Gibraltar has a name.*

Moorish Castle **

The Tower of Homage, built in 1333, dominated the approach to Gibraltar for centuries and still bears the scars of 10 sieges that took place between the 14th and 15th centuries. In 1540, the Moorish castle, which probably dates back to the eighth century, was where the people of Gibraltar took refuge from Barbarossa's marauding pirates, who virtually destroyed the town.

Apes' Den **

Halfway up the Rock are the famous **Barbary apes**, two colonies of tailless macaques found in the wild only in **Morocco** and **Algeria**. Legend has it that as long as the apes are here, Gibraltar will belong to the British, and the monkeys as a result have always been well cared for, although they roam free. Accustomed to tourists, the monkeys are quite tame but will bite if provoked.

St Michael's Cave **

This vast cavern was first inhabited by Neolithic Man and is used today for concerts and fashion shows. Cathedral Cave, the largest chamber, was believed to be bottomless, which gave rise to the legend that Gibraltar was linked to Africa by an underground tunnel. The cave was supposed to be used as a military hospital in World War II, although it never was, and a new series of caverns was discovered as the rock was blasted out. The tour today descends 63m (207ft) below the entrance past eerie limestone formations.

Gibraltar Town ***

Gibraltar's compact town, surrounded by old walls, gates and casements, is best explored on foot. **Casemates Square**, entrance to Main Street and now a busy area of shops and pubs, was once used for public executions. The **Changing of the Guard** takes place outside the governor's residence – ask at the tourist office for details. Gibraltar's **museum** is now located in what is considered the best preserved Arab bathhouse in Europe, with star-shaped skylights and Roman, Visigothic and Moorish columns.

A 15-minute film shown throughout the day tells the story of Gibraltar, after which visitors may wander through the museum which contains artefacts from the stone age, right up to weapons used in the Great Siege. A scale model, built in 1865, shows life in Gibraltar in the 18th century.

Fortifications

Fortifications all around the town date back to various eras. The 16th-century wall was built in the time of Charles V, while **King's Bastion** was reinforced by the British in 1775 and was the point from which red-hot shot was fired at Spanish ships in the Great Siege, piercing their hulls and causing them to sink. **Line Wall** has been a defensive wall since 1704, built on a Moorish sea wall. All the land to the west has been reclaimed. **Southport Gate** is comprised of three gates from different eras, built respectively by Charles V, Queen Victoria, and to commemorate the referendum in 1967, when Gibraltar voted overwhelmingly to retain its links with Britain.

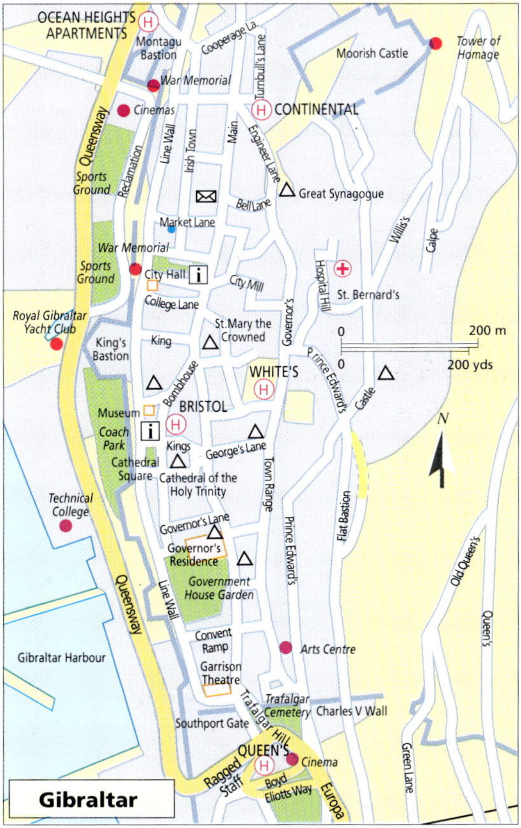

Gibraltar

MARINE LIFE

One of the most pleasing sights in summer is **dolphins** playing with boats and leaping out of the water in Gibraltar Bay. Three species live here: the **common dolphin**, the **striped dolphin** and the large **bottle-nose dolphin**. Although they are wild, the shoals will chase boats and dive under the bows. Several companies now operate dolphin safaris. Occasionally, visitors will be lucky enough to spot **pilot** or **killer whales** and less frequently, **sperm whales**. Sadly, whales have almost died out here now as a whaling station established in Algeciras earlier this century decimated the population. **Loggerhead turtles** can also be found on remote beaches.

MOROCCO SURVIVAL GUIDE

• Buy the ferry or hydrofoil ticket from a travel agent, not from one of the hustlers at Algeciras docks, who add an unofficial 'commission'.
• Change money into Moroccan *dirhams* once through Moroccan customs, as the exchange rates are much better than in Spain.
• Never accept an offer of a guided tour from a stranger, even if they are wearing a badge and carry identification.
• Do not even entertain the idea of buying drugs as penalties are severe.
• Agree a price in advance with taxi drivers.
• Do not wander around Tangier alone after dark.

NORTH AFRICA

Up and down the Costa del Sol, travel agents sell shopping trips to **Tangier** in Morocco and to a lesser extent, to **Ceuta**, one of two tiny enclaves of Spanish territory in North Africa. While Tangier can in no way be compared with the beautiful imperial cities of **Fez** and **Marrakech** further south, it still provides a brief taste of Morocco and a good opportunity for shopping in the market.

Ferries make the two hour, 30-minute crossing from **Algeciras**, a busy port west of Gibraltar, several times a day. An important strategic point, guarding the entrance to the Mediterranean like Gibraltar, **Tangier** has in its time been occupied by Greeks, Phoenicians, Vandals, Arabs, Berbers, Almoravids, Almohads, Spanish, Portuguese, British and French. Not surprisingly then, a number of different influences in the architecture are noticeable, although the medina, the old town by the port, is distinctly Arabic.

The maze of narrow streets around the busy **Grand Socco** Square is a great place to bargain for carpets, leather bags and jackets, brassware, herbs, spices and wooden carvings and is full of the sights and smells of Africa. Visitors may not enter the mosques, although the opulent **Dar el-Makhzen Palace** (open Wednesday–Monday 09:00–13:00, 15:00–18:00) houses the excellent museums of Moroccan art and antiquities. **Ceuta**, a Spanish colony 1½ hours from Algeciras by ferry, is a pleasant but unexciting town; its biggest attraction is tax and duty-free status, hence the large number of shops.

TARIFA

An easy day trip from the main resorts of the Costa del Sol, Tarifa is the southernmost point of Spain and supposedly the windiest place in Europe, hence its popularity as a **windsurfing centre**. Surf shops line the main street and the long, sandy beaches and Atlantic rollers are a riot of coloured sails for most of the year. A young, lively culture has sprung up in the town as a result, although the beaches are less attractive to sunbathers as the winds are too strong to sit comfortably on the sand for long.

Tarifa has a deeper, more tragic past than this and dates back to Roman times. Important Roman remains of the city of Baelo Claudia, built in AD171, have been found at the nearby village of **Bolonia** and are considered among the best preserved in Spain. Tarifa itself is built around a 10th-century **Moorish castle** now named after Guzmán el Bueno (the good), commander of the town in 1292 when it was under siege by Moorish attackers. A Christian traitor had taken Guzmán's young son prisoner and threatened to kill him if the commander did not surrender the town. Guzmán threw his own dagger to the Moors and the son was killed, but the town did not fall.

HOW TO HAGGLE

Haggling is a way of life in Morocco and should be considered part of the culture, not a threat or an insult to visitors. First, decide what you think an item is worth after shopping around. Expect to pay about one fifth of the 'official' price but start lower than this and prepare to meet in the middle. Be polite but firm.

Vendors will try every trick known to man: expressions of horror, disbelief, stories of hardship – but don't be fooled. Some will offer mint tea, the traditional Arabic way of doing business and if you are genuinely interested in making a purchase, it is polite to accept, but keep haggling. Sometimes it pays to shrug politely and walk away as a final tactic – if the vendor is still keen to sell, he will soon follow you with a lower offer.

Opposite: *Day trips to Morocco are a paradise for bargain hunters.*
Left: *Tarifa's high winds attract windsurfers from all over Europe.*

Western Costa del Sol At a Glance

BEST TIMES TO VISIT

Peak season for golf at this end of the coast, where the most prestigious courses are located, is the **winter** months of **January** to **April** and any visitor expecting to play should book well in advance. **Summer**, like anywhere else on the Costa del Sol, is hot and dry, so the best months for touring and sightseeing are **March** to **June**. **Winters** tend to be mild, although Gibraltar often has a misty cloud hanging over it during the cooler months.

GETTING THERE

Two main gateways to this end of the coast are Málaga and Gibraltar. Málaga is served by **Iberia** and other airlines from most European capitals and Gibraltar has daily services from London with **GB Airways**. Travelling by road, the area is connected to the rest of Spain by an efficient **motorway system** to Málaga and Cádiz, northwest of Gibraltar. From Málaga, the **N340** highway extends all the way along the coast to Cádiz.

GETTING AROUND

Car rental agencies have offices in all major resorts. Visitors can pick up a car in Gibraltar for use in Spain, although it must be returned to Gibraltar. Driving in Gibraltar is on the right, as in Spain. The **Portillo** bus company operates up and down the coast, although anybody visiting Gibraltar will have to disembark in La Línea and walk the short distance to the border. The easiest way of getting around Gibraltar is by taxi or guided tour; parking is very difficult. Algeciras, west of Gibraltar is the departure point for ferries and hydrofoils to Morocco. Operated by **Transmediterranea,** they leave twice a day in summer, making the crossing in one hour. Ferries depart every two hours and take 2½ hours. Tickets can be bought from any travel agency. There are also six ferries and six hydrofoils a day from Algeciras to Ceuta and a service from Gibraltar to Tangier.

WHERE TO STAY

Costa del Sol
LUXURY

Hotel Atalaya Park, Ctra. Nac 340 km168, 29680 Estepona, tel: (95) 288-4801, fax: (95) 288-5735. Well located four-star with excellent sporting and golf facilities.

Golf Hotel Guadalmina, Hacienda Guadalmina, 29678 S. Pedro Alcántara, tel: (95) 288-2211, fax: (95) 288-2291. Modern design, easy access to Puerto Banús and Marbella. Ideally located for Nueva Andalucía golf courses.

Hotel Paraiso, Ctra. Nac. 340 km167, 29680 Estepona, tel: (95) 288-2019. Behind Estepona with views of coast and El Paraiso golf course.

Kempinski Resort Hotel Estepona, Ctra. de Cádiz km159, 29680 Estepona, tel: (95) 211-3306, fax: (95) 211-3465. Attractive new hotel, lavish spa and sandy beach.

MID-RANGE

Hotel El Pueblo Andaluz, Ctra. Nac 340 km172, 29600 S. Pedro Alcántara, tel: (95) 270-0597, fax: (95) 278-9104. Attractive hotel built around old Andalucían house near beach.

BUDGET

Hostal El Pilar, Plaza Las Flores, 29680 Estepona, tel: (95) 280-0018. Small, cozy hostel in pretty setting.

Gibraltar
LUXURY

White's Hotel, Governor's Parade, Gibraltar, tel: (350) 70-500, fax: (350) 70-243. Centrally located, deluxe hotel managed by Holiday Inn.

The Rock Hotel, Europa Road, Gibraltar, tel: (350) 73-000, fax: (350) 73-513. Set in tropical gardens above the town, with spectacular views.

MID-RANGE

Bristol Hotel, 10 Cathedral Square, Gibraltar, tel: (350) 76-800, fax: (350) 77-613. Central location with pool and lovely garden.

Caleta Palace Aparthotel, Catalan Bay, Gibraltar, tel: (350) 76-501, fax: (350) 42-143. Large, modern hotel outside town on Catalan Bay.

Western Costa del Sol At a Glance

Tarifa
LUXURY
Hotel Balcón de España, Ctra. Nac. 340, km77, 11380 Tarifa, tel: (95) 668-4326, fax: (95) 668-0472. Located just out of town with pool and horse riding. Summer only.

MID-RANGE
Hurricane Hotel, Ctra. Nac. 340, km77, 11380 Tarifa, tel: (95) 668-4919. Relaxed atmosphere attracting a lot of serious windsurfers.

WHERE TO EAT

There are fewer restaurants west of Marbella, although Estepona has some good *tapas* bars. Food in Gibraltar is mainly British or international.

Costa del Sol
Mesón El Coto, El Madronal, Ctra. de Ronda, tel: (95) 278-6688. Mountain setting five minutes from coast. Barbecues and game specialities.
Bar Mesón El Cordobes, Plaza de las Flores 16, Estepona, tel: (95) 280-0737. Good *tapas* bar in town centre, open until 22:00.
El Carnicero, La Cancelada, Ctra. Cádiz km165, tel. (95) 278-5123. Friendly, rustic place outside Estepona. The restaurant specializes in Spanish country cooking.
Cabo Mayor, Club Marítimo Hotel, Puerto Sotogrande, Cádiz, tel: (95) 679-0390. Memorable gourmet dining in Puerto Sotogrande.

Gibraltar
Admiral Collingwood's, The Square, Marina Bay, tel: (350) 79-241. English food with Sunday carvery.
Bunter's Bar Restaurant, College Lane, tel: (350) 70-482. Reliable English and vegetarian dishes.
Bourbon Street, 150 Main Street, tel: (350) 43-765. New Orleans Cajun cooking and Spanish *tapas*.
La Bayuca, 21 Turnbulls Lane, tel: (350) 75-119. Gibraltar's oldest restaurant. Scottish beef and apple pie are the specialities.

Tarifa
Hurricane Hotel, Ctra. Nac. 340, km77, 11380 Tarifa, tel: (95) 668-4919. Original cuisine with plenty of salads and fish. Value for money.

SHOPPING

Most shops in Gibraltar are British, including **Marks & Spencer** and **Woolworths**. Prices are tax-free, making Gibraltar a popular shopping excursion for perfumes, spirits, jewellery, cashmere and porcelain. Gibraltar currency is the pound, tied to the British pound, although most places take pesetas and sterling. Shoppers should be careful to change Gibraltar pounds back before they leave, as the currency is not accepted in the UK. For a different kind of shopping, the *souks* of Tangier sell carpets, spices, brass, leather and handicrafts, all subject to heavy bargaining. Ceuta also enjoys duty-free status.

TOURS AND EXCURSIONS

Most tour companies have pick up points in Estepona or San Pedro for excursions to Granada, Sevilla, Jerez, Córdoba, Ronda, Nerja, Gibraltar, Tangier and Fuengirola market. Tours of Gibraltar are operated by **Bland Travel**.
Andalucían Adventures, Estepona, tel: (95) 280-4438.
Taxi tour of Gibraltar, tel: (350) 42-400.
Bland Group, Cloister Building, Irish Town, Gibraltar, tel: (350) 77-012.

USEFUL CONTACTS
Municipal Tourist Office, P. Marítimo Pedro Manrique S/N, Estepona, tel: (95) 280-0913.
GB Airways, Cloister Building, Gibraltar, tel: (350) 79-200, fax: (350) 76-189.
Gibraltar Tourist Board, Duke of Kent House, Cathedral Square, Gibraltar, tel: (350) 74-950, fax: (350) 74-943.
Santa Marina Polo Club, Sotogrande, tel: (956) 79-6464.
Car rental in Gibraltar
Avis, Bland Ltd, Bayside Road, tel: (350) 75-552, fax: (350) 76-189.
Budget Rent-a-Car, Regal House, Queensway, tel: (350) 79-666.

5
Ronda, the White Towns and Jerez

The mountainous interior of the Costa del Sol is an area of raw, natural beauty, the romantic *pueblos blancos* (white towns) sprinkled across craggy landscapes, eagles and vultures wheeling above the highest peaks. **Ronda**, the most famous of all the White Towns, perches precar-iously on the lip of a deep gorge while others cling to cliffs or nestle high in blind valleys.

Many of the towns in this wild country have the suffix '**de la Frontera**', or 'of the frontier', which explains their sometimes unlikely positions. The frontier in question was the edge of **Moorish Andalucía** in the almost 800 years of Moorish rule here (711–1492) and these tiny towns, each dominated by a fortified castle, formed the first line of defence between the Moors and the Christian lands beyond. Each town has a typical Moorish configuration – a tangle of narrow streets and alleyways below the castle and small, whitewashed houses opening inwards to shady patios.

Beyond the mountains, the verdant countryside opens out into a wide chequerboard of plains, golden with wheat and sunflowers. This is the edge of the floodplain of the Guadalquivir River and further west is the famous sherry triangle and the ancient town of **Jerez de la Frontera**, capital of sherry country. The *ruta de toros* (route of the bulls) bisects this landscape and closer towards Jerez, huge fighting bulls can be seen in the fields, tended by cowboys on horseback. The prize bulls of these herds are very much in demand and the best are selected for the rings of **Sevilla** and **Málaga**.

DON'T MISS

*** Jerez: sherry-tasting in the traditional *bodegas*.
*** Ronda: divided by a deep gorge and home of one of Spain's oldest bullrings.
*** Pueblos Blancos: the beautiful, white hilltop towns of Andalucia.
** Royal Andalucian School of Equestrian Art: see the dancing white horses.
** Arcos de la Frontera: a town perched on the edge of a sheer cliff.

Opposite: *Many of the White Towns were built in strategic defensive positions by the Moors.*

RONDA

One of the oldest cities in Spain and certainly one of the most dramatic locations, Ronda perches 750m (2461ft) above sea level on an inland plateau, slashed in half by a deep gorge, **El Tajo**. The city is about an hour's drive from the Costa del Sol through rugged mountain scenery, the **Serranía de Ronda**, which opens out onto plains of sunflowers in spring.

Ronda has a colourful and romantic past and in popular Spanish history is associated with bandits and bullfighters. The bullring here is one of the oldest in Spain and was where the great matador **Pedro Romero** lived, fought and died. Bandits, meanwhile, roamed the mountains in the last century, robbing wealthy tourists headed for Ronda on their Grand Tour of Europe. In this century too, Ronda has held a fascination for writers and bullfighting enthusiasts from far afield. **Ernest Hemingway** wrote two books featuring the city: *For Whom the Bell Tolls* and *Death in the Afternoon*. Actor **Orson Welles** is buried here.

Ronda dates back to Moorish times, when it was an important cultural centre of al-Andalus, richly adorned

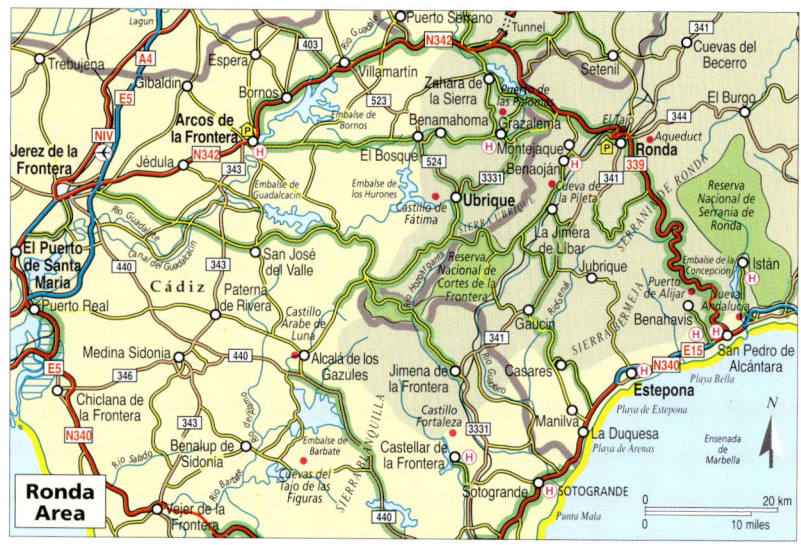

with palaces and mosques. The Moors managed to defend the city against the Christians right up until 1485, just seven years before the *reconquista* was completed with the conquest of Granada. In those days, just the part of the town known as **La Ciudad**, south of the gorge, existed. The new part of the town, **El Mercadillo**, sprung up after the Christian reconquest when taxes imposed on La Ciudad were so high that its residents were forced to set up a new quarter.

The main road from the coast enters the city via two ancient gates: the Moorish **Puerta de Almocabar**, which in the 13th century was the main gateway to the castle; and the 16th-century **Renaissance Gate** built by Charles V. Much of the Moorish layout of La Ciudad remains; a maze of narrow streets with whitewashed houses interspersed with some grand Renaissance mansions. The **Santa María la Mayor** church on Plaza Duquesa de Parcent was the city's original mosque in the 13th century, later converted to a Catholic church with a belfry being installed on top of the old minaret. Traces of Arabic inscriptions can still be seen inside. The **Minaret of San Sebastián** close by is all that remains of another 14th-century mosque.

Palacio de Mondragón **

Located on the **Plaza de Campillo** in the Moorish quarter, this palace was built by Abomelic, King of Ronda, in 1314 and housed subsequent Moorish rulers before Ferdinand and Isabella, the Catholic kings, converted it for their own use after the reconquest. Much of the original stucco work and coloured mosaics remain around the spacious patios with their horseshoe arches. The roof terrace looks out over the broad plains below. Open Monday–Friday 10:00–19:00; weekends and holidays 10:00–15:00.

Above: *Ronda perches on the lip of a deep gorge, El Tajo.*

BEST TIMES TO VISIT

Jerez is hotter than the coast in summer and cooler in winter. July and August temperatures reach 38°C (100°F). Ronda and the White Towns are always a few degrees cooler than the coast and in winter receive some rain and occasional snowfall, although on the many sunny winter days, the air in the mountains is beautifully clear. Special events include the **Jerez Horse Fair** in May, when everywhere is fully booked; the **Jerez Wine Harvest** in September; and the *goyesca* bullfighting festival in Ronda in September, when the town is very busy.

Above: *The three bridges spanning Ronda's gorge are stunning feats of architecture.*
Opposite: *More than 200 years old, Ronda's bullring is known as the cradle of modern bullfighting.*

A TASTE OF RONDA

Ronda produces a number of dishes unique to the area. Look out for *morcilla rondeña*, the town's famous black pudding: a blood sausage seasoned with cloves, pepper, cumin, oregano, paprika, coriander and garlic. The local cheese, generically branded *queso de Málaga*, is a yellowish goat's cheese, cured and preserved in olive oil. Cake shops all over the town sell *yemas del tajo*, rich cakes made with egg yolk and sugar. In the city's restaurants, try trout from the mountain streams of the Serranía de Ronda, grilled with almonds, and Ronda raspberries marinaded in the sweet Málaga wines.

La Casa del Rey Moro *

This 18th-century palace overlooking the gorge from the **Calle Santo Domingo** was not actually the home of a Moorish king as its name implies, although it is built on Moorish foundations. The house itself is not open to the public but nonetheless has an interesting story: a 14th-century underground stairway, *la mina* (the mine), leads from the garden to the river flowing through the gorge. Christian slaves were used in times of siege to form a water supply line, hoisting buckets up the stone staircase.

Palacio del Marqués de Salvatierra **

Located on the same street, this Renaissance mansion is open daily to the public except when the Salvatierra family is in residence. Carved figures of Inca Indians at the entrance are a reminder of the way people adorned their houses at the time of the discovery of the New World.

El Tajo Gorge ***

Three bridges span the El Tajo Gorge. The original Moorish structure, **Puente de San Miguel**, looks down on the well-preserved 13th-century Arab baths (open Tuesday–Saturday 10:00–14.00, 16:00–19:00; Sunday 10:00–14:00). Next to it, the **Puente Viejo** was built in 1616. The **Puente Nuevo**, the new bridge, dates back to 1788 and has dramatic views of the gorge and the plains beyond. The gorge itself, not surprisingly, has a gruesome past. One of its victims was the architect of the Puente Nuevo, who fell to his death while reaching for his hat, blown away by a gust of wind. Apart from countless suicides, Republican sympathisers were thrown into the gorge during the Spanish Civil War by Franco's troops and in the 18th century, injured horses from the bullring were flung over the cliff.

Plaza de Toros ***

Located on the Plaza de España in the Mercadillo section of Ronda, the bullring (open 10:00–18:00 in winter; 10:00–20:00 in summer) is one of the oldest and most revered in Spain. Dating back to 1785, it was the stage upon which

Pedro Romero, considered the founder of modern bullfighting, evolved the graceful style of fighting bulls on foot rather than horseback, an art which is still emulated today. The artist Goya painted Romero and his colleagues and in their honour, a special festival is held each year in early September, the *goyesca*, featuring only the country's best matadors, dressed in 18th-century costumes, and the finest bulls. A small museum inside has bullfighting memorabilia and posters advertising the very first *corrida* in the ring.

North of the bullring a leafy park, the **Alameda del Tajo**, has two *miradors* with breathtaking views from the clifftop, looking out over the plains.

HEMINGWAY IN RONDA

American author Ernest Hemingway, famous for his crisp, laconic writing style, worked as a newspaper correspondent in Spain throughout the Spanish Civil War, during which time he was inspired to write the novels *For Whom the Bell Tolls* and *The Sun Also Rises*. For a while, he lived in a suburb of Málaga on a *finca* (ranch) which now serves as the region's hotel training school.

Hemingway befriended the great bullfighter Antonio Ordóñez, a relationship which fuelled his fascination with bullfighting. His novel, *Death in the Afternoon* is a magnificent prose about the drama of the bullring.

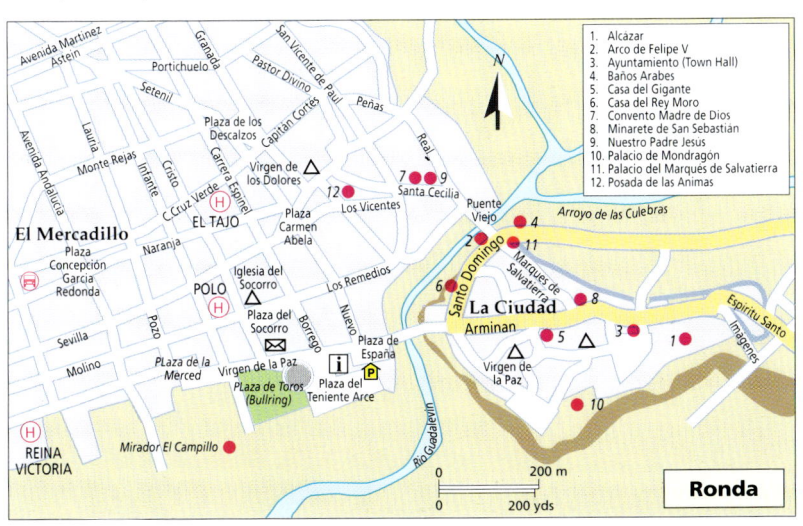

1. Alcázar
2. Arco de Felipe V
3. Ayuntamiento (Town Hall)
4. Baños Arabes
5. Casa del Gigante
6. Casa del Rey Moro
7. Convento Madre de Dios
8. Minarete de San Sebastián
9. Nuestro Padre Jesus
10. Palacio de Mondragón
11. Palacio del Marqués de Salvatierra
12. Posada de las Animas

Ronda

Above: *Zahara de la Sierra has one of the most dramatic locations of all the* pueblos blancos.

THE GREEN GORGE HIKE

Before Zahara village is another walking trail, this time requiring about three hours and walking boots. Stop at the km8 marker of the **CA531** and follow the trail to the left, which leads up to the **Garganta Verde**, a dramatic canyon through which the River **Bocaleones** flows in the winter. A colony of vultures lives here and Spanish ibex and hare may also be spotted.

The trail continues to the **Ermita de la Garganta**, a cave with stalactites and stalagmites, which takes over an hour to reach. From here, it is necessary to turn round; the path continues but only experienced climbers should try.

THE WHITE TOWNS

Mountain roads in the Serranía de Ronda are well sign-posted and in reasonable condition but in order to make the most of a day out, try not to be overambitious with distances. Spend some time on foot instead, trying short hikes and exploring the villages.

Much of the hiking country in this area is designated nature reserve and permits are needed from the **Agencia de Medio Ambiente** to walk here (*see* p. 87). Permits can be picked up in Grazalema.

Scenic Drive:
Ronda–Grazalema–Zahara de la Sierra–Ronda

Take the **C339** from the coast road just beyond Marbella and follow the signs to Ronda, a spectacular drive which takes about an hour. Cross through Ronda and continue on the **C344** until the left turn to **Grazalema**, a further 13km (8 miles).

Grazalema is a sleepy, little village that appears almost to be suspended from a bare cliff face in the heart of the **Sierra de Grazalema Parque Natural**. Grazalema is the wettest spot in Spain, the mountains trapping cool air from the sea, and it is this high altitude combined with frequent rainfall that sustains the rare *pinsapo* fir, a tree which only grows in this area.

Many people use Grazalema as a starting point for **hikes** in the *pinsapo* forests and the sun-dappled cork oak woods. The village's main square is usually busy with walkers and old people sitting under the shade of maple trees to observe the scene. The village is also famous for its **hand-woven blankets** and a couple of shops around the square sell the soft woollen products of a small factory outside the town. In the peaceful back streets, colourful window boxes provide a brilliant contrast against the white walls; restaurants serve local specialities like wild trout stuffed with mountain ham, and onion soup with cheese and walnuts.

From Grazalema, continue up through the valley to the turn-off for the **CA531**, signposted **Zahara** and **Puerto de las Palomas**. This breathtaking mountain pass is the highest in Andalucía and weaves its way up the side of a sheer rock face through the *pinsapo* forest. The views from the top at 1350m (4429ft) are awe-inspiring, rugged mountains with green, wooded valleys in between them and dusty, golden fields rolling away on the plain to the western horizon. Golden eagles and griffon vultures wheel overhead. A trail on the left marks the beginning of the **Itinerario del Pinsapar**, the walking path through the *pinsapo* forest. With a permit it is possible to follow the path for an hour or so, although the full length of the trail takes four hours and ends in nearby **Benamahoma**.

Left: *Grazalema is the wettest spot in Spain, according to records.*

CUEVA DEL GATO

An alternative to driving in this area is to hike from the pretty village of Benaoján to the **Cueva del Gato**, an impressive cave from which a small stream emerges, filling an ice-cool pool at the cave mouth, ideal for a swim in summer. Take the old road from **Benaoján** towards the railway station and turn left onto the road which leads to Ronda. Cross the railway line and continue towards **Ronda** and turn left onto the track crossing the River Guadiaro, heading northeast towards the craggy scenery of the **Sierra del Algarrobo**. The cave mouth is more than 10m (33ft) high and a large colony of bats hangs inside. Allow two hours in each direction for the walk.

Once over the pass, the road makes a hairpin descent towards a conical hill topped by a solid-looking Moorish castle. The sugar cube houses of **Zahara de la Sierra**, a village designated a national monument, spill down the opposite side but soon come into view.

Zahara was built by Moors in the eighth century and was an important stronghold until its capture by the Christians in the late 15th century. A dirt track next to the church leads up to the 800-year-old castle ruin, with sweeping views over the cluster of red roofs below and the reservoir in the background.

From Zahara, take the **C339** along the banks of the lake back to Ronda and on to the coast.

Scenic Drive:
Ronda–Cueva de la Pileta–Gaucín–Casares–Manilva
This route covers the eastern **Serranía de Ronda** with a detour to see the prehistoric rock paintings in the Cueva de la Pileta (open 10:00–13:00, 16:00–18:00). Drive through Ronda and take the turn-off to Benaoján and from there, follow the signs to the cave. Inside the cave are primitive

rock paintings of animals that roamed this area in 25,000BC, made all the more atmospheric by the fact that there is no lighting and the one-hour tour is conducted by lantern.

Continue south to **Jimena de Libár**, a village overlooked by the remains of a Moorish castle. At the junction with the **C341**, turn right and follow the signs for Gaucín, 19km (12 miles) away. **Gaucín** is one of the most beautiful of the **White Towns**, spilling over the saddle of a hill dominated by a Moorish fortress. The views over the coastal plain to Gibraltar and Morocco are breathtaking. While there is little of historical interest in the town, it is pleasant to wander around and have a drink.

At the western end of the village, an unnumbered road slopes steeply downward, the left fork leading to **Casares**, another immaculate *pueblo* suspended from a hillside beneath its castle. Casares allegedly takes its name from Julius Caesar, who used to favour the sulphuric springs down the mountainside outside Manilva. The spa is ruined now but the strange-smelling water continues to gush out.

Because of its proximity to the coast – just 18km (11 miles) from Estepona, Casares is less remote than the other White Towns and has a sprinkling of expatriates' homes and the craft shops and restaurants that spring up as a result. The Moorish Alcázar is built on Roman ruins; scramble up to the top for stunning views of the coast.

Above: *Casares has views of the mountainside and the Mediterranean.*
Opposite: *Gaucín's Moorish fortress overlooks the town's whitewashed houses and red-tiled roofs.*

ARCOS DE LA FRONTERA

Two hours drive from Marbella over the craggy Serranía de Ronda and down onto rolling hills, Arcos de la Frontera is the furthest west of the White Towns. High above the River Guadalete, the whitewashed village spills down a sheer limestone cliff, its warm sandstone monuments glowing in the sun.

Inhabited first by Romans, then by Moors, Arcos fell to the Christian forces in 1264, the defeat of such an important strategic post signifying the beginning of the end for the Moors in Andalucía. All the important monuments today are within easy walking distance of one another, the walls of the **Moorish castle** and the towering Gothic-Mudéjar Church of **Santa María de la Asunción**, which is built on the site of a former mosque, forming two sides of the main **Plaza de España**. The church was built between the 16th and 18th centuries and has a beautiful Plateresque south façade with a tall, but unfinished bell tower. A *mirador* (viewing point) on the open side of the square looks out over the chequered plains. The town's interesting *parador* (state-run hotel) is also located on this square.

Further into the old town, through narrow, shaded streets is the Gothic church of **San Pedro**, leaning precariously out over the steep cliff face. The 15th-century altar inside is worth a look. For an even higher vantage point, climb the tower. Other monuments worth the short walk are the **Casa Cuna**, once a synagogue, and the **Iglesia de la Coridad**, a 16th-century church on the square of the same name.

For a large town, Arcos is surprisingly sleepy and in the old section there are relatively few places to eat or interesting streets in which to stroll. Most of the restaurants are located at the foot of the hill, which is also the best place to park.

JEREZ DE LA FRONTERA

Just 20km (12½ miles) inland from the coast in the province of Cádiz, a day trip from the Costa del Sol, Jerez de la Frontera is famous throughout Spain for two reasons: wine and horses. The two go hand in hand: wealthy wine growers who have lived in the area for generations set up vast country estates and were quick to adopt country pursuits like breeding thorough-

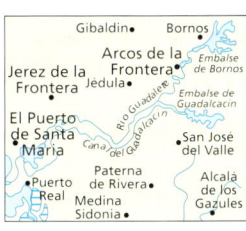

Opposite: *The church of San Pedro in Arcos de la Frontera, perched on the edge of a sheer cliff.*
Left: *The narrow streets of Jerez are deserted in the midday sun.*

breeds to match their lifestyle. Jerez horse and wine society is notorious among Andalucíans for its airs and graces.

Over 200 sherry *bodegas* (wine cellars) are located in the town and visitors can tour the cool, musty cellars of famous producers such as **González Byass**, **Sandeman**, **Williams and Humbert**, **Harvey** and **Domecq**. Jerez also has an interesting old Jewish quarter, the **Barrio de Santiago**, which is pleasant to wander around.

Twice a year, the whole town turns out for events which have reached international acclaim: the **Jerez Horse Fair** and the **Wine Harvest**. In May, stock farmers bring out their very best for a week of *haute école* dressage displays, *Vaquera* (the unique Andalucían dressage), jumping, carriage driving and thoroughbred showing, accompanied by the usual consumption of *jerez* and *tapas*, bullfighting and flamenco dancing. The wine harvest takes place in September, an occasion for similar celebrations as the grapes are crushed.

BULLFIGHTING OVERSEAS

Spain is not the only country in the world to have a bull-fighting season. **Mexico** stages regular *corridas* throughout the winter, while **Peru** has its season in the autumn, from March to May. Bullfights also take place in **Venezuela**, **Columbia** and **southern France** on feast days. **Portugal** has a bull-fighting following as enthusi-astic as Spain's, although the bull is not killed in front of the spectators, but in the slaughterhouse afterwards.

In Portugal, the matador is mounted on a highly trained horse and he drives the *banderillas* into the bull's shoulders. The Spanish, how-ever, do not count Portugal as a bullfighting nation.

Sherry Bodegas ★★★

Many of the *bodegas* close down in August but for the rest of the year, tours, in English, are run on most days. Advance booking is essential. Each *bodega* has a tradition of celebrity autographs on its dusty old barrels and visitors to González Byass, for example, will spot the signatures of General Franco and Orson Welles. The tours demonstrate the sherry- and brandy-making process and end with a tasting, based on the saying: 'if you don't have a *copa* by eleven, you must have eleven at one'. The wine is aerated by pouring it with a flourish from heights of one metre or more into tiny glasses known as *copitas*.

Royal Andalucían School of Equestrian Art ★★★

The Royal Andalucían School of Equestrian Art is located next to a 19th-century palace in a beautiful park, **Recreo de las Cadenas**, and is regarded as one of the top dressage schools in the world. The Spanish thoroughbred is a brave, intelligent breed with graceful movements and a characteristically long, flowing mane and tail and is ideally suited to the intricate movements of *haute école*, or High School dressage. The spectacular **Sinfonía Caballo**, which

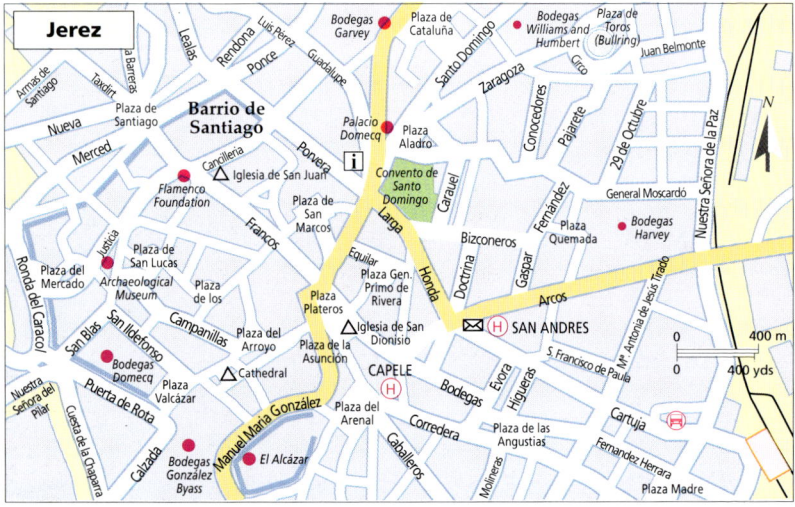

the Spanish describe as a 'horse ballet', takes place every Tuesday and Thursday at 11:00 and must be booked well in advance. The performance is similar to that of the Spanish Riding School in Vienna. Alternatively, watch the horses in training on other weekdays and tour the stables and tack room. Open Monday–Wednesday and Friday 11:00–13:00.

Above: *The church of San Salvador, where the celebration of the wine harvest begins each September.*

Jerez Town ★★

Most of the major sights are within walking distance of the **Plaza del Arenal**, the town's main square. Like most cities in Andalucía, Jerez was once occupied by Moors and the **Alcázar**, the old Moorish castle (open 10:00–14:00, 16:00–18:00, mornings only in August), was built by Almohads in the 11th century. The original tower and some of the Arab baths remain.

East of the **Plaza del Arenal**, the **San Salvador**, or **La Colegiata** Church is a mixture of Gothic and Renaissance styles and has a separate bell tower. Facing the church is the **Barrio de Santiago**, a fascinating maze of narrow streets that was once the gypsy quarter of the city, hemmed in by remnants of the old city wall. As well as several interesting Gothic churches and a small archaeological museum, this is the location of the **Andalucían Flamenco Foundation,** housed in an elegant 18th-century mansion. Concerts and exhibitions are held here throughout the year and an audio-visual presentation takes place on the hour on weekday mornings, explaining the history and art of flamenco (open Monday–Friday 10:00–14:00).

Further north, close to the School of Equestrian Art on Calle Cervantes is the **Museo de Relojes** (clock museum) of Jerez (open Monday–Saturday 10:00–14:00), with more than 300 antique clocks and watches, all functioning and said to be one of Europe's most important collections.

EL PUERTO

El Puerto de Santa María is a typical town of **Cádiz** province, with a well-preserved old section, beautiful beaches and lively nightlife. Some of the best **seafood** in Andalucía can be found in El Puerto, as the locals call it, in the string of simple beach cafés at **La Puntilla** and **Valdelgrana** and along the quayside of the Guadalete River in the **Ribera del Marisco**. The popular **Romerijo** bar here serves enormous portions of fresh seafood, the shells and claws of which are thrown into a bucket on each table. Noisy, crowded and exceptional value, it makes a great night out. The traditional **drinking port** for the sherry houses of Jerez also comes from here.

Ronda, the White Towns and Jerez At a Glance

BEST TIMES TO VISIT

During the **spring** and early **summer**, the mountain scenery is most attractive. Between June and September, when the coast is at its hottest, the slightly cooler temperatures at altitude can be a welcome relief, although the plains around Jerez and Arcos de la Frontera can be even hotter at this time. The **winter** months are often cloudy with some rain and snow in the mountains.

GETTING THERE

Public bus and coach services (**Autobus Portillo**, tel: (95) 287-2262) operate between the coast and the White Towns, although a car allows more freedom to explore some of the remote villages. Jerez has an international airport, served by **GB Airways** from London and by domestic flights from major Spanish cities. Jerez and Ronda are also accessible by train from Málaga and the coast.

GETTING AROUND

The White Towns are ideal for exploring by car, on foot, by mountain bike and on horseback and facilities exist for each. Roads across the Serranía de Ronda, including the smallest single-track mountain roads, have good surfaces and villages tend to be well signposted, although the highest passes may be icy in winter. The best road from the Costa del Sol is the **C339** from San Pedro de Alcántara, which is curves a lot but in good condition. Footpaths, often following ancient mule tracks across the mountains, are sometimes poorly marked and certain difficult hikes need orienteering expertise. Much of the area is protected national park and walkers require a permit from the **Agencia de Medio Ambiente**, Spain's environmental protection agency. For information on horseriding holidays, contact Andalucía's equestrian association, AETEA, c/Julio César 2, 1d, 41001 Sevilla, tel: (95) 421-1311.

WHERE TO STAY

Ronda
LUXURY

Parador de Ronda, Plaza de España S/N, 29400 Ronda, tel: (95) 287-7500, fax: (95) 287-8188. Stunning views over the Tajo Gorge from the *parador's* clifftop position. Rustic Andalucían cuisine, including plenty of game.

Hotel Reina Victoria, c/Jerez 25, 29400 Ronda, tel: (95) 287-1240, fax: (95) 287-1075. Turn of the century hotel with sweeping views from clifftop.

MID-RANGE

Hotel El Tajo, c/Doctor Cajal 7, 29400 Ronda, tel: (95) 287-4040, fax: (95) 287-5099. Comfortable three-star in Mercadillo section.

Hotel Polo, c/Mariano Soubirón 8, 29400 Ronda, tel: (95) 287-2447, fax: (95) 287-2449. Three-star hotel near the bullring and gorge.

BUDGET

There are plenty of rooms to rent around the Calle Jerez in the Mercadillo area.

Hotel Virgen de los Reyes, c/Lorenzo Borrego 13, 29400 Ronda, tel: (95) 287-1140. Close to the bullring. All rooms have private bathroom.

White Towns
LUXURY

Parador de Arcos de la Frontera, Plaza del Cabildo S/N, 11630 Arcos de la Frontera, tel: (956) 700-500, fax: (956) 701-116 Located on the main square in the old town with stunning views across the plains.

MID-RANGE

Hotel el Molino del Santo, Bda. de la Estación, 29370 Benaoján, Málaga, tel: and fax: (95) 216-7151. Converted mill with rustic furnishing, 30 minutes' drive from Ronda.

Hostal Grazalema, Olivár, Ctra. Comarcal, 344, Cádiz tel and fax: (956) 132-213. Small hotel in traditional style overlooking the village.

Hotel el Convento, c/Maldonado 2, 11630 Arcos de la Frontera, tel: (956) 700-233. Family-run hotel in old convent building. Excellent restaurant.

Ronda, the White Towns and Jerez At a Glance

Hotel Los Olivos, c/San Miguel 2, 11630 Arcos de la Frontera, tel: (956) 700-811, fax: (956) 702-018. Converted town house with pretty patio.

Jerez de la Frontera
LUXURY
Hotel Royal Sherry Park, Avda. Alvaro Domecq 11, 11405 Jerez de la Frontera, tel: (956) 303-011, fax, (956) 311-300. Modern four-star in quiet residential area.
Hotel Jerez, Avda. Alvaro Domecq 35, tel: (956) 300-600, fax: (956) 305-001. Expensive but luxurious four-star further from the centre than the Royal Sherry Park.

MID-RANGE
Hotel Capele, c/Corredera 58, 11402 Jerez de la Frontera, tel: (956) 346-400. Modern hotel close to sherry *bodegas*. Lively bar and restaurant.

BUDGET
Hostal San Andres, c/Morenos 12, tel: (956) 340-983, fax: (956) 343-196. Pleasant hostel near the sherry *bodegas*.

WHERE TO EAT
Ronda
Parador de Ronda (*see* Where to Stay). Regional specialities in a dramatic setting.
Pedro Romero, Virgen de la Paz 16, tel: (95) 287-1110. Famous establishment opposite the bullring with bullfighting theme. Serves regional specialities.

Restaurante Jerez, Plaza Teniente Arce 2, tel: (95) 287-9028. Meat dishes including *rabo de torro* (oxtail), the local favourite.
Don Miguel, Villanueva 4, tel: (95) 287-1090. Good, wholesome food and stunning location, built next to the Puente Nueve.

White Towns
Hostal Las Truchas, Avenida de Cádiz 1, 11670 El Bosque, tel: (956) 716-061. Rustic hostel in peaceful location. Try the trout stuffed with *jamón serrano* (cured ham).
Casa de las Piedras, c/Las Piedras, Grazalema, tel: (956) 132-014. Local specialities including asparagus with wild mushrooms and trout stuffed with ham.
Restaurante el Convento c/Marqués de Torresoto 7. Local specialities in an atmospheric setting.
Parador de Arcos de la Frontera, (*see* Where to Stay). Has *menu degustación* with nine or ten small courses of local dishes.

Jerez de la Frontera
El Abaco, Avda. Alvaro Domecq 11, 11405 tel: (956) 30-3011, fax: (956) 31-1300. Intimate restaurant in hotel grounds, fresh seafood.
La Mesa Redonda, c/Manuel de la Quintana 3, tel: (956) 340-064. Good value and an extensive menu. Closed Sundays, holidays and summer.

TOURS AND EXCURSIONS

Book **sherry *bodega*** visits in advance, direct or through hotels. **Domecq**, tel: (956) 331-800, **Fernando de Terry**, tel: (956) 857-700, **Gonzáles Byass**, tel: (956) 340-000, **Harvey's**, tel: (956) 151-030, **Luis Caballero**, tel: (956) 861-300, **Osborne and Duff Gordon**, tel: (956) 855-211, **Williams & Humbert**, tel: (956) 346-539.
The **Royal School of Equestrian Art** needs to be booked well in advance, tel: (956) 311-100. Performances Tuesdays and Thursdays (excluding holidays) at 12:00 and rehearsals other weekdays. Travel agents up and down the coast operate tours to Ronda. Try **Pullmantur**, tel: (95) 238-4400 (Torremolinos). Within the Nature Park of Grazalema, **Turismo Rural de Bocaleones** operates mountain biking, trekking and horseriding tours, tel: (956) 123-114.

USEFUL CONTACTS

Tourist information in **Jerez**, Alameda Christina 7, tel: (956) 331-150, fax: (956) 331-731. **Ronda**, Plaza de España 1, tel: (95) 287-1272. **Arcos de la Frontera**, Pso. de Boliches 24, tel: (956) 701-560. **Agencia de Medio Ambiente** (environment agency for walking permits), c/Las Piedras 11, Grazalema, tel: (956) 132-230.

6
Eastern
Costa del Sol

East of Málaga, the Costa del Sol is a complete contrast to the busy west. This is Málaga's market garden: dense orchards of peach, cherry, custard apple and pomegranate interspersed with row upon row of greenhouses. Vines are grown high in the hills and further east, sugar cane is farmed. The shoreline is dotted with *atalayas*, or watchtowers, dating back to the days of Charles V when the coast was subject to frequent invasions by Barbary pirates. The towers were also a means of communication between one village and the next.

The holiday resorts scattered between **Málaga** and **Almería** are less commercial than their western cousins and consist mainly of apartment blocks serving as weekend homes for the inhabitants of Málaga and **Granada**. Fishing boats are pulled up on the rocky beaches, having unloaded their morning catch of sardines and anchovies. Whitebait used to be a valuable source of income, but because of depleting stocks, fishing was banned over a decade ago. Some of the little coves are deserted, except, perhaps, for one beach bar. The stony seabed means the water is a wonderful translucent shade of turquoise.

This stretch of the coast forms the southern border of two provinces, Málaga and Granada. Granada's share of the shore is known as the **Costa Tropical** because of its balmy climate. Beyond **Motril**, an industrial town close to Almería, the green fields fade into barren desert and unique mountain scenery which looks like the set of a spaghetti western. To the surprise of many, it is and the film sets are open to the public.

DON'T MISS

*** Granada's Alhambra:** one of the most important Moorish palaces in the world.
** The Royal Chapel in Granada:** burial place of Isabella and Ferdinand, the 'Catholic kings'.
** Nerja's Balcón de Europa:** the promenade at the heart of the coast's most charming resort.
** The Caves of Nerja:** containing the largest stalactite in the world.
* **Frigiliana:** twice winner of Andalucía's 'most beautiful village' award.
* **Mini Hollywood:** the set of *A Fistful of Dollars*.

Opposite: *The Alhambra in the early evening light.*

RUM

A surprising fact about the **Costa del Sol** is that it introduced rum to the **West Indies**. The only sugar cane grown in Europe comes from **Málaga** and **Granada** provinces and it was from here that the cane, which is not native to the West Indies, and its distilling techniques were taken to the New World in the 16th century. Rum is still produced in Spain today, in **Cádiz** and around **Motril**, in **Granada** province.

Below: *Nerja's elegant promenade, the Balcón de Europa, is a popular place for a stroll.*

FROM MALAGA TO NERJA

Immediately outside Málaga lie a series of unspectacular resort towns, frequented mainly by local people who keep weekend apartments here. **Rincón de la Victoria** and **Torre del Mar** have, however, recently been relieved of lorries thundering past, thanks to the extension of the Málaga-Almería motorway, a stretch of road badly needed to open up this part of the coast to tourism and commerce.

The most attractive part of this stretch of coast is just inland. The market town of **Vélez-Málaga**, just 4km (2½ miles) into the fertile hinterland, has a Moorish section overlooked by a ruined castle and some attractive Mudéjar features in the church of Santa María la Mayor. **Torrox itself**, 4km (2½ miles) inland from Torrox Costa, is a pretty, whitewashed hill village that once formed an important centre on the silk trading route from Granada. While there is little of the old town remaining today, it makes a pleasant coffee and browsing stop.

NERJA

The only genuinely international resort along this coastline, 51km (32 miles) from Málaga, Nerja is a bustling, easy-going place with a more informal feel than the neon and glitz of its western counterparts. The name 'Nerja' comes from the **Moorish** word *naricha*, meaning 'rich in water' and the town is surrounded by peach and pomegranate groves.

Eastern Costa del Sol

Despite its development into a holiday destination in the 1960s, Nerja has managed to avoid high-rise development and most of the accommodation is situated in the pretty centre or in whitewashed villas on the hills behind. A car, or at least a bicycle, is a good idea here, as some of the best and most deserted beaches are a short distance away.

Ensenada de Málaga

Nerja's most famous attraction is the **Balcón de Europa**, a short, palm-lined promenade jutting out over a couple of small coves, with sweeping views of the coast in either direction. A couple of 400-year-old cannons point out to sea.

The old part of the town clusters around the promenade and spills over the edge of the cliff, some hotels having uninterrupted views of the coast. Twisting, narrow streets are lined with souvenir shops and cafés, the latter filled with Nerja's many foreign residents enjoying a 'morning *café con leche*. By night, the centre comes alive with *tapas* bars and restaurants, fairy lights hung over the narrow streets. Every year, a song and dance festival takes place in August, when the town is packed with would-be flamenco stars and classical guitarists.

Two festivals are also worth attending. On 15 and 16 May, the whole town celebrates the pilgrimage of **San Isidro**, an occasion when everybody dresses in traditional costume and parades out into the countryside to the shrine of the saint. On 16 July, in common with every other village along the coast, Nerja celebrates the festival of the **Virgen del Carmen**, the patron saint of fishermen.

MALAGA WINE

Wine-growing capital of the Málaga region, **Cómpeta** is a typical Andalucian village 20km (12½ miles) inland from **Algorobbo Costa** – white cube houses clinging to a steep hillside. Undulating vineyards surround the village, where **Moscatel** grapes are grown to produce Málaga's small but prized crop of sweet dessert wine.

A few places in the village offer free tasting – look out for the ***degustacion*** signs – but the best time to visit is 15 August, the **Noche del Vino**, or annual wine festival, when the wine is free and the whole village turns into one big party.

Nerja Caves ★★★

Nerja achieved international fame in 1959 when a group of local schoolboys stumbled on some of the most dramatic underground limestone formations in Europe, complete with Neolithic paintings and tools dating back 27,000 years to 25,000BC. Now open to the public, the **Cuevas de Nerja** are worth a visit for the dramatic caverns dripping with magnificent stalactites and bizarre rock formations, including one joined column which is said to be the world's largest.

Sadly, the rock paintings are not on view to the public although excellent photos of them are displayed in one of the galleries along with tools, artefacts and fragments of pottery. During a *feria*, concerts of anything from jazz or rock to flamenco dancing are held in the largest cave and have proved very popular.

Frigiliana ★★★

High in the hills behind Nerja is Frigiliana, a gem of a village which won an award in 1992 as the most beautiful in Andalucía. After the *reconquista*, Frigiliana became a **Morisco** settlement, inhabited by **Moors** who had been forced to convert to Christianity. Eventually all the Moors, including the Moriscos, were expelled from Spain and the sad tale of their persecution is told by coloured, ceramic murals dotted around the **barrio morisco**, the immaculately preserved, old part of the village.

Despite the fact that it is a popular tourist attraction, Frigiliana retains all its charm – donkeys clattering through the narrow streets and gypsies calling out to the elderly householders, offering items for sale. Every balcony is a riot of colour and scarlet geraniums tumble out of ceramic pots framing each doorway. There are shops and bars in the lower part of town, the only area navigable by car, selling ceramics, mountain honey, olive oil and wine. For the best view, climb up to the *mirador* (lookout point), offering spectacular views of the orchards and coast. There is a little bar and barbecue at the top.

Almuñécar ★

East of Nerja is Almuñécar, the weekend resort for the inhabitants of Granada. The resort has a rather exotic feel about it – a substantial seaside town nestling among a circle of hills, one of which is topped by an imposing Moorish castle. Dense, tropical orchards almost seem to encroach on the town. A couple of kilometres to the west, the new **Puerto del Este** marina development has an almost Italian appearance with its expensive yachts gleaming at the base of a steep, terraced cliff adorned with stately cypress trees and luxury villas.

Founded by the Phoenicians and later inhabited by Romans and Moors, Almuñécar has worked hard to preserve its heritage. The **Castillo de San Miguel**, built around the time of Charles V, sits on top of a rocky headland which divides the resort's twin bays and occupies the site of the former Moorish castle. There is nothing inside apart from the graveyard but the views from the *mirador* are spectacular. At the base of the hill, an **ornithological park** contains beautifully coloured parrots and rare birds, housed amidst tropical foliage (open 10:00–14:00, 16:00–18:00 in winter; 11:00–14:00, 18:00–21:00 in summer).

Above the main square, **Plaza Ayuntamiento**, there is a small **Archaeological Museum**, open Monday–Saturday 10:30–13:30, 16:00–18:00 (October–April); 10:30–13:30, 18:00–20:00 (May–September), located in the **Cueva de los Siete Palacios**, a structure believed to have been a Roman water reservoir. It houses important local finds, including an Egyptian vase dating from the 17th century BC.

Almuñécar is a lively place by night with restaurants lining the seafront promenade, the **Paseo Puerta del Mar** and some good *tapas* bars in the *casco antiguo* (old town). Cultural life thrives here with the occasional spontaneous flamenco and annual **Andrés Segovia** guitar competition, which attracts a nationwide following.

Salobreña *

The village of Salobreña, about 13km (8 miles) east of Almuñécar, enjoys an unusual location, tumbling down the side of a massive rock outcrop jutting out of the patchwork sugar cane fields of the flat coastal plain. The name Salobreña comes from *Salambo*, the Syrian goddess of love, revealing the village's **Phoenician** origins. Later, Moorish inhabitants added an impressive **Alcázar**, still in a good state of repair, with sweeping views across the plain from its crenellated towers. The village is worth a detour from the main road to visit this and the 16th-century church at the foot of the hill, **Nuestra Señora del Rosario**, which stands on the site of a former Moorish palace.

Opposite: *Frigiliana is a perfectly preserved Moorish village and has won awards for its beauty.*

TYPICAL TAPAS

Aceitunas •
olives, served everywhere
Albóndigas •
meatballs in sauce
Boquerones fritas •
fresh anchovies, tossed
in flour and fried
Champiñones al ajillo •
mushrooms with garlic
Croquetas •
croquettes of chicken or fish
Jamón serrano •
cured ham, often served with
slices of cheese (*queso*)
Mejillones •
mussels, usually steamed
Patatas bravas •
sauteéd potatoes served in
a spicy tomato sauce
Pimientos •
sweet peppers, sometimes
stuffed with cheese
Riñones al Jerez •
kidneys served in sherry
Tortilla •
Spanish omelette, cooked
with potatoes, ham and
vegetables and served cold

BOABDIL

Between Motril and Granada is the **Puerto del Suspiro del Moro** – the Pass of the Sigh of the Moor, 850m (2789ft) above sea level. **Boabdil**, the last Moorish ruler to surrender is said to have looked back and wept here in 1492, having exchanged his beloved city for a smaller kingdom in the Alpujarras. His mother, however, was scathing: 'Weep like a woman for what you have failed to defend like a man', were her cruel words.

GRANADA

Two hours' drive northeast of Málaga, Granada is home to one of Andalucía's most exquisite Moorish palaces, the beautiful, red-walled **Alhambra**, set against a fairy-tale backdrop of the snow-capped peaks of the **Sierra Nevada**. In addition, the city houses many important Catholic monuments and was the birthplace of one of Spain's most popular poets, **Federico García Lorca**.

The temptation is to spend as much time as possible admiring the magnificent Alhambra but Granada also has some fascinating areas to explore; the old silk market around the **Capilla Real** and the **Albaicín**, a cluster of impossibly narrow streets in the old Arab quarter.

Granada is significant to Andalucían history in that it was the last of the Moorish kingdoms to surrender to Los

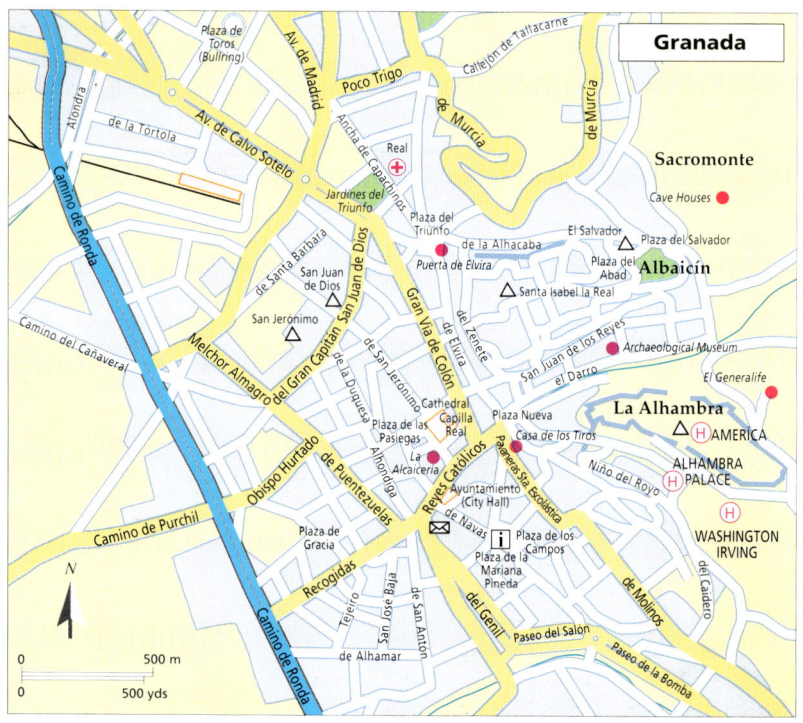

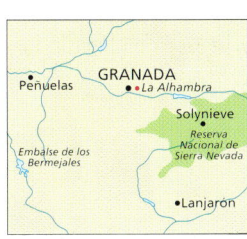

Left: *The best view of Granada's old Arab quarter, the Albaicín, is from the ramparts of the Alhambra.*

Reyes Católicos (Catholic kings), Ferdinand and Isabella. The **Moors** had ruled the city since AD711 and while other kingdoms in al-Andalus were falling to the advancing Christian armies throughout the 13th and 14th centuries, Granada had resisted. But the dynastic marriage of Ferdinand of Aragón and Isabella of Castile in 1479 and the vast power it produced was too much for the Moors.

In 1491 Ferdinand and Isabella marched on the city with an enormous army, holding it under siege for seven months until **Boabdil**, the last Moorish king, handed over the keys to the city in January 1492, the same year **Christopher Columbus** sailed to the West Indies.

The Alhambra ★★★

The name 'Alhambra' comes from the Arabic *Al Qal'a al-Hamra*, meaning the 'red fort'. Mohammed Ibn al-Ahmar, the first of the Nasrid kings, built the **Alcazaba**, the oldest part of the Alhambra, in the 9th century. The **Royal Palace** was completed by Mohammed V in the 15th century, by which time the Alhambra had *souks*, a Turkish bath, three palaces and running water diverted from the River Darro.

Ferdinand and Isabella lived in the palace after the conquest of the city but changed little; it was their grand-son, **Charles V**, who destroyed a whole series of rooms in 1526 to build a palace of his own right in the middle of the intricate columns and mosaics. He never lived in the palace and it remained incomplete until Felipe II built another floor. The palace now houses a small **Fine Arts Museum** and the **Museum of Hispano-Moorish Art**.

FEDERICO GARCIA LORCA

One of the greatest contributors to Andalucian literature, Federico Garcia Lorca was born in **Granada** in 1898. He grew up on a farm just outside the city and in 1928 achieved national fame with his book, *El Romancero Gitano*, a collection of gypsy ballads. Inspired by gypsy tradition and his passion for Granada and its surrounds, Lorca went on to write *Bodas de Sangre* (Blood Wedding) and *Yerma*, his two best-known plays, and roamed Spain with his own travelling theatre group.

Lorca was always outspoken about cultural issues in Granada and was a Republican sympathizer and homosexual. His vicious execution by Fascist terrorists in July 1936, at the start of the **Spanish Civil War**, however, has never been understood, and to this day his body has not been found.

Right: *Once a kitchen garden, the Generalife today is a manicured oasis.*
Opposite: *Water played an important role in Moorish architecture.*

Touring the Alhambra

There are three main sections to explore in the Alhambra: the **Alcazaba** and the palace of Charles V; the **Casa Real**, or Royal Palace; and the **Generalife Gardens**. Guided tours take two hours, although it is easy to spend longer.

The main entrance is through the **Puerta de la Justica**, one of the old gates to the castle, dating back to 1348, bearing the symbol of a key, representing Allah opening the gates to Paradise. An outstretched hand represents the five symbols of **Islam**: diligent prayer, fasting, the giving of alms, pilgrimage to Mecca and oneness with Allah. Little remains of the original **Alcazaba** other than walls and foundations, although the watchtower **Torre de la Vela** has magnificent views across the Darro Valley to the jumble of the Albaicín, the old Arab quarter of the city, clinging to the hillside and out over the plains beyond. A bare rock face behind the Alhambra appears to be peppered with holes – these are the gypsy caves of Sacromento, still inhabited today.

Casa Real ***

The Royal Palace is the Alhambra's priceless gem. There are three sections: an outer area in which the king would receive ordinary people; a second for entertaining more elite visitors and the third for the king, his harem and the royal household. Every wall in the massive palace

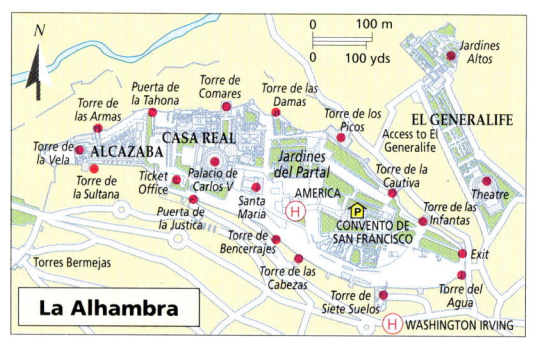

La Alhambra

is decorated with brilliantly coloured mosaics, which reflect different shades as the sun passes overhead, moulded walls with inscriptions from the Koran in relief and intricate wooden ceilings of Lebanese cedar, depicting the heavens.

When the Moors lived in the palace, there would have been little furniture, just woven rugs and cushions on the cool floors. Mosaics were used for the lower part of the walls because they were cool to lean against and the ceilings are so elaborate because the Moors spent much of their time reclining and gazing upwards. Stalactite-like formations under the arches depict the cave in which the prophet **Mohammed** wrote the Koran.

The first section opens out into the **Patio de los Arrayanes**, the Court of Myrtles, a beautiful, tranquil courtyard with a rectangular goldfish pool and fountain flanked by scented myrtle hedges. At each end of the pool is a key shape, again representing the key to paradise. Water is an important feature of Moorish architecture; first, it was needed for washing in before praying but second, it represented an oasis in the desert from which the Moors had originated.

Off the patio are two magnificent rooms, the **Sala de la Barca**, with a wooden ceiling shaped like an inverted boat hull and the **Salon de los Embajadores**, the Hall of the Ambassadors. Here, every centimetre of wall is covered by inscriptions from the Koran and poetry, some in the ancient Kufic script. This was the room where the king would receive his ministers, always sitting with his back to the light so they could only see him in silhouette. The ceiling, made of 8000 pieces of wood interlocking

like a puzzle, depicts the seventh heaven and was one of the last parts of the palace **Boabdil,** the last Moorish ruler, would have seen, as it was in this room that he received Ferdinand and Isabella and agreed to surrender the city of Granada.

Above: The patio of the lions in the Alhambra.

Patio de los Leones *

One of the most tranquil parts of the inner palace is the sunlit **Patio de los Leones**, the lion patio. Twelve lion statues around a central fountain were believed to have been donated to the Moors by the Jewish people of Granada, representing the 12 tribes of Israel. Each lion is marked with a Star of David. Four channels flowing from the fountain represent four rivers in heaven – of honey, milk, water and wine – and the 124 slender, intricate columns around the patio again represent the seventh heaven, as the numbers one, two and four make seven. Interestingly, each column incorporates a lead ring halfway up, as protection against the occasional earth tremors that shake the city.

One of the rooms off the patio, the **Sala de los Abencerrajes**, is named after a noble family, the men of which were slaughtered here by Boabdil's father, Abu al-Hassan, because he suspected one of them of being in love with one of his wives. Despite its gruesome story, this is one of the most beautiful rooms in the palace, with an exquisite ceiling of silvery blue stalactite vaulting and a refreshing, tinkling fountain catching the light from windows in the dome.

The **Sala de las dos Hermanas** (Room of the Two Sisters) is equally stunning, with the only remaining, original wooden window grille, through which the Sultana used to observe life in the palace.

The Generalife ★★★

A footbridge leads from the Alhambra to the Generalife, the leafy gardens and patios around the summer palace of the kings. Tall avenues of cypress trees, ornamental fountains and pools and luxuriant flowerbeds radiating violet, orange, vermillion and dusky rose make this a perfect place to sit and reflect on the beauty of the Alhambra, at the same time admiring the views across the city and Albaicín.

In the 14th century, the Generalife served partly as a kitchen garden for the palace. Orange and almond trees, mint, figs and pomegranates would have grown here, a far cry from the manicured perfection of today.

Capilla Real ★★★

Located in the **Alcaiceria**, a former Moorish silk market in the city centre, the **Royal Chapel** is an impressive Gothic structure with an elaborate Renaissance altar, built by Ferdinand and Isabella in 1504 as a mausoleum for themselves, having apparently said that they wanted to live forever in the last Arab kingdom (open 10:30–15:00 October–March, 11:00–13:00 Sundays and holidays; 10:30–15:00 and 16:00–19:00 April–September, 11:00–13:00 Sundays and holidays).

The burial tombs themselves are simple caskets in a tiny crypt although a lavish monument to the monarchs and their daughter **Juana the Mad** and son-in-law, **Felipe the Handsome**, stands above, carved in marble in the style of Michelangelo by Italian artist **Domenico Fancelli** in 1517. Panels along the side depict scenes of Christ and the Apostles. The figures of King Ferdinand and Queen Isabella look very similar but Isabella's head – allegedly heavier than her husband's because she was more intelligent – sinks much further into her stone pillow.

Below: *Queen Isabella's wish was to be buried forever in this chapel in the last Arab kingdom.*

A magnificent gilded grille guards the high altar, carved from wood and covered with gold-leaf and illustrating scenes from the lives of Ferdinand and Isabella including the enforced baptism of the captured Moors. Several items are on display in the sacristy, including Ferdinand's sword and Isabella's sceptre and a silver and gilt jewellery box that was handed, full of gold coins, to Columbus by Isabella to finance his expeditions. A heavy tapestry was hung from a tree by the Christians to create a temporary place of worship when they first entered the city. Isabella's collection of paintings is also exhibited, including work by **Botticelli**, and medieval Flemish artists **Bouts** and **Van der Weyden**.

The Albaicín ★★★

Full of atmosphere, the Albaicín is the city's old Arab quarter, clinging precariously to a hillside facing the Alhambra. Little has changed over the years and most of the cobbled streets are too narrow for cars to negotiate. Iron grilles across the doors of the tiny whitewashed houses reveal hidden *carmens*, or town gardens – exquisite patios bursting with vines, lemon trees, pomegranates,

Below: *The Alhambra looks down on to the roof-tops and patios of the Albaicín quarter.*

and a fountain usually tinkling at the centre. From the **Mirador de la Morayma**, the highest point, the views of the Alhambra glowing red in the late afternoon sun are breathtaking. The little square is a place to sit and contemplate the view and listen to old gypsy women clicking castanets and humming arias from *Carmen*.

Sacromonte *

Outside the Alhambra, the barren hillside off the **Camino de Sacromonte** is dotted with natural cave openings, which until recently were inhabited by gypsies. Most of the gypsies now live in the houses below, many of which simply form the front of a cave hollowed further into the soft rock. The area is not particularly safe because of petty thievery and bag-snatching. It has fallen off the tourist map but in daylight merits a brief stroll for the odd surprise.

'Authentic' gypsy flamenco evenings continue to be a tourist attraction in these cave houses, events which are highly commercial but nonetheless have a certain atmosphere. Beware, however, of the cost of hidden 'extras' – souvenir pictures, castanets and tapes of the music – and don't walk around the area alone at night.

Above left: *Many of the streets of Albaicín are too narrow for cars.*
Above right: *Windowsills are adorned with pot plants.*

EAST COAST FESTIVALS

Almería: Romería of the Virgen del Mar on the first Sunday in January and fiesta in the last week of August.
Almuñécar: Fiesta of the Virgen de la Antigua, 15 August. Custard apple fiesta on 12 October, with tropical fruit tasting.
Competa: La Noche del Vino (wine festival), 15 August.
Nerja: Fiesta of San Miguel, 9–12 October. Romería of San Isidro on 15 May. Ballet performances in the caves, second half of August.
Salobreña: Fiesta of Nuestra Señora del Rosario, 4–7 October.

Above: *The crenellated walls of Almería's Alcazaba are remarkably well preserved.*
Above right: *Around Almería, the coast is sparsely populated.*

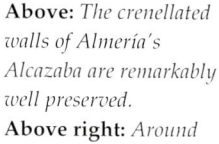

ALMERIA POTTERY

Pottery has always been of fundamental importance in arid Almeria province because of the need to store water effectively. Several towns produce a unique style of earthenware using techniques which have not changed for centuries. In **Vera**, the clay is almost white and the shapes inspired by Arab, Phoenician and Byzantine forms. **Albox** produces elegant water pitchers and **Sorbas** produces rustic ceramics and tiles. **Níjar** and **Tabernas** also specialize in unglazed pottery, usually for holding water. All of these styles can be found in Almeria's shops and markets.

ALMERIA

The easternmost city of the Costa del Sol, Almería is surrounded by mountains – the green Sierra Nevada to the west and the desert-like Sierra Alhamilla to the northeast. The city itself is modern and sprawling but with some pleasant old areas and a spectacular **Alcazaba** dating back to the 10th century, when Almería was an important port serving the Moorish stronghold of Granada.

Named al-Mariyat, the 'mirror of the sea', the city flourished until 1488 when the Christians expelled the Moors and shared out all their land and possessions among themselves. Almería fell into a decline, rocked by a series of violent earthquakes and only began to recover during the last century as the arrival of the railway allowed commercial exploitation of the province's rich mineral reserves.

The Alcazaba **

The fortified walls of the old citadel have been remarkably well preserved and features such as the **Keep** and the towers of **La Justicia** and **Los Espejos** remain intact. In the second compound are the crumbling remains of an old mosque, later used as a church. High on the hill, the inner section was reinforced by the Catholic kings and is guarded by three towers. Try to visit at sunset – the views from the gunpowder tower over the city and the gypsy quarter are spectacular.

Cathedral ★★

Almería's cathedral has the unusual appearance of a fortress, having been deliberately reinforced because of the constant attacks on the city by Barbary pirates around 1524, when it was built. The Renaissance and Gothic façade has four towers made from huge blocks of stone which once held cannons. Inside are paintings and sculpture by 16th- to 18th-century artists.

Mini Hollywood ★★

If the barren mountains beyond **Almería** look familiar, it is because they have appeared in many Hollywood films. Bearing a remarkable resemblance to the deserts of Arizona and the Middle East, Almería was first 'discovered' by director Sir David Lean in 1962, who shot *Lawrence of Arabia* here. Two years later Italian director Sergio Leone made *A Fistful of Dollars*. The spaghetti western was born and Almería was put on the map.

Soon, the idea of making westerns in Almería took off. The climate – an average of 22°C (72°F) year-round, the 11 hours of daylight in the summer months, the lack of rainfall – and cheap peasant labour made this part

of Spain an ideal location. But by the mid-1970s the western had had its day. The owners now make money out of it as a tourist attraction and visitors can take tours around this and a second lot; ride western-style, order 'two fingers of Red Eye' at the Saloon bar and, every two hours, enjoy a staged shoot-out.

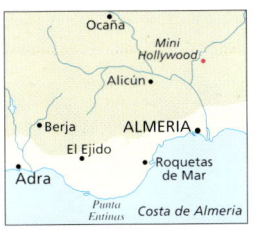

Left: *Clint Eastwood and Marianne Koch starred in* A Fistful of Dollars, *shot on location in Almería.*

Eastern Costa del Sol at a Glance

BEST TIMES TO VISIT

Unlike the western half of the Costa del Sol, the east is largely seasonal and is at its most lively during the **summer** months. The season begins around **May** and extends to **October**, between which months most villages celebrate their annual festivals. Granada is busy throughout the year but is probably at its most beautiful in **spring**, when the Sierra Nevada forms a snowy backdrop. **November** is also a good month to visit, when the trees are changing colour, the air is clear and the first snows have fallen in the mountain.

GETTING THERE

Málaga is the main **airport** serving the Costa del Sol with **international** and **domestic** services. Granada and Almeria also have airports with good connections to other Spanish cities. Charter flights from the **UK** operate into **Almería**.

GETTING AROUND

Regular excursions operate to Granada from all the resorts along the coast and the city is easily accessible by road, either along the **highway** from Málaga or across the Sierra Nevada. Local **buses** operate between the resorts on the coast and the mountain villages. **Car rental** offices in Nerja and Granada.

Granada is easily accessible by **rail** from most Spanish cities – tel: (958) 271-272 for up-to-date details. Buses also operate to **Almuñécar**, **Málaga** and **Sevilla**. Contact **Alsina Graells Sur**, tel: (958) 185-010, for the current schedules and fares.

WHERE TO STAY

Nerja
LUXURY
Hotel Parador de Nerja, Alumuñécar 8, 29780 Nerja, tel: (95) 252-0050, fax: (95) 252-1997. *Parador* located just outside town in lush gardens with views from clifftop.
Hotel Monica, Playa Torrecilla, 29780 Nerja, tel: (95) 252-1100, fax: (95) 252-1162. Large, modern four-star hotel with good facilities.

MID-RANGE
Hotel Balcón de Europa, Balcón de Europa 1, 29780 Nerja, tel: (95) 252-0800, fax: (95) 252-4490. Arguably the best address in town with really stunning views and a lift to the beach.

BUDGET
Hotel Portofino, Puerto del Mar 2, 29780 Nerja, tel: (95) 252-0150. Small beach hotel within walking distance of the centre.
Hostal Avalon, Punta Lara, 29780 Nerja, tel: (95) 252-0698. Tiny, charming hostel situated just outside Nerja near the beach.

Granada
LUXURY
Hotel la Bobadilla, Finca la Bobadilla, Loja, tel: (958) 321-861, fax: (958) 321-810. Five-star country estate about 30 minutes west of Granada.
Hotel Alhambra Palace, Peña Partida 2, 18009 Granada, tel: (958) 221-468, fax: (958) 226-404. Romantic views and Moorish design within easy walking distance of the Alhambra.
Parador Nacional San Francisco, Real de la Alhambra, 18009 Granada, tel: (958) 221-440, fax: (958) 222-264. A beautiful *parador* in an old, gracious convent inside the Alhambra.

MID-RANGE
Hotel Washington Irving, Paseo de Generalife 2, 18009 Granada, tel: (958) 227-550, fax: (958) 228-840. Faded but charming hotel in the Alhambra where the celebrated American author used to live and write.

BUDGET
Pension Florida, c/San Miguel 33 , Nerja, tel: (952) 520-743. Comfortable and good value for money. Situated just around the corner from the bus station.
Hotel América, Real de la Alhambra 53, 18009 Granada, tel: (958) 227-471, fax: (958) 227-470. Small hotel in Alhambra, cheaper than the *parador*.

Eastern Costa del Sol at a Glance

WHERE TO EAT

Nerja

Casa Luque, Balcón de Europa, Nerja, tel: (95) 252-1004. Elegant old house in a clifftop location with lovely gardens. Local food and occasional flamenco dancing.
La Capilla del Mar, c/de la Cruz 16, Nerja, tel: (95) 252-1993. Popular restaurant specializing in game.
Meson Antonio, c/Diputación 18, Nerja, tel: (95) 252-0033. *Tapas* and *raciónes* a speciality.
El Capricho, c/Carretera, Otivar, tel: (958) 645-025. Rustic village restaurant inland from Almuñécar serving local specialities including chicken with apples and roast meats.
Bar el Mirador, Frigiliana. Bar and barbecue at the top of Frigiliana village, with breathtaking views.

Almuñécar

There are countless inexpensive places to eat but the best *tapas* bars and fresh fish restaurants are on the seafront of the old town.
Casa Paco, Playa Velilla seafront, tel: (956) 285-451. Rather expensive but excellent seafood; the custard apple tart is the house speciality.

Granada

A *tapas*-bar crawl makes a good alternative to dinner in Granada's old city. Start somewhere around the

Puerta Real, **Plaza Nueva** or the riverside **Paseo de Padre Manjón**.
Ruta del Veleta, Ctra. de Sierra Nevada, km5.4, tel: (958) 486-134. Spanish gourmet cooking in atmospheric restaurant 5km (3 miles) from city on the Veleta road. Closed Sundays for dinner.
La Alacena de las Monjas, Plaza Padre Suarez 5, tel: (958) 224-028. Original Spanish cuisine in the vaults of a 15th-century convent, central Granada.
Mirador de Morayma, C7 Pianista Garcia Carrillo 2, Barrio de Albaicín, tel: (958) 228-290. Mouthwatering Granada specialities in romantic old house with walled gardens and breathtaking views of the Alhambra.

TOURS AND EXCURSIONS

Excursions from this end of the coast are similar to those from the west, although day trips to **Gibraltar** and **Morocco** involve very early starts. **Halcon Viajes** operates half-day tours from Almuñécar to Frigiliana and full day excursions to Granada and the Alpujarras.

The caves at Nerja are 3km (2 miles) out of town and can be easily reached on foot. As a flow control measure, independent visitors to the **Alhambra** in **Granada** will be allocated a time slot in which they must enter the grounds. Check opening times with the tourist board.
Alhambra, tel: (958) 227-527.
Patronato de la Cueva de Nerja, tel: (95) 252-9520, fax: (95) 252-9646 (check opening times as they often vary).
Halcon Viajes, Plaza de Madrid 1, Almuñécar, tel: (958) 880-513.

USEFUL CONTACTS

Guides and Tourist Informers' Association of Granada, Puerta del Vino, S/N 18009 Granada, tel: (958) 229-936.
Tourist information Nerja, Calle Puerta del Mar 2, Nerja, tel: (95) 252-1531.
Tourist information of Granada, Pl. Mariana Pineda 10, 18009 Granada, tel: (958) 226-688.
Tourist information Almuñécar, La Najarra, Avda. Europa S/N, 18690, tel: (958) 631-125.

GRANADA	J	F	M	A	M	J	J	A	S	O	N	D
AVERAGE TEMP. °C	7	8	10	14	17	22	26	26	22	17	12	7
AVERAGE TEMP. °F	45	46	58	57	63	72	79	79	72	63	54	45
HOURS OF SUN DAILY	5	5	5	8	10	11	11	11	8	7	6	5
RAINFALL mm	100	100	100	63	50	25	13	-	13	75	100	125
RAINFALL in	4	4	4	2.5	2	1	0.5	-	0.5	3	4	5
DAYS OF RAINFALL	8	8	7	6	5	2	1	-	1	7	8	9

7
Beyond the Coast

Inland from the Costa del Sol are two of Spain's greatest cities, **Sevilla** and **Córdoba**, packed with architectural treasures. Both are accessible as a day trip, albeit a long one, but an overnight stay would do either justice. You should spend an evening in Sevilla to soak up the heady atmosphere of a balmy summer night and explore the *tapas* bars and flamenco *tablaos* of the old quarter, or wander round the exquisite Mezquita in Córdoba and enjoy the city's easy-going lifestyle.

Between Granada and the eastern stretch of the coast is the **Sierra Nevada**, Spain's highest mountain range, its peaks blanketed in snow for much of the year. One of the proud boasts of the Costa del Sol is that visitors can ski in the morning and enjoy the setting sun by the beach in shirtsleeves, as the mountains are only 35km (22 miles) inland from the **Mediterranean**. Better, though, to spend a few nights of your holiday in one of the **white villages** of the **Alpujarras**, the dramatic foothills of the Sierra with steep, green terraced slopes and cascading rivers which have cut deep gorges into the rock.

SEVILLA

Romans, **Moors** and **Christians** and now modern man have all shaped Sevilla's magnificent monuments. Columbus set out from here in 1492 on his journey of discovery to the New World. Five hundred years later, billions of pesetas were spent in commemoration on Expo '92, the futuristic pavilions of which gleam in the sun on the **Isla de la Cartuja**.

DON'T MISS
*** Sevilla Cathedral: the largest in the world.
*** La Giralda Tower: for a great 360° view of Sevilla.
*** La Mezquita: Córdoba's magnificent Arab mosque.
*** Las Alpujarras: breath-taking mountain scenery and unspoilt villages.
** Barrio Santa Cruz: *tapas* and *fino* in this area of Sevilla.
** Flamenco: sit in a Sevillan *tablao* and be entertained.
* Sierra Nevada: spend a day's skiing in mainland Spain's highest mountains.

Opposite: *Sevilla's magnificent Giralda Tower is visible from miles around.*

La Giralda ★★★

The beautiful La Giralda, a **Moorish minaret** dating back to the eighth century, has become the symbol of Sevilla and is all that remains of the mosque built by the Arab conquerors. The name Giralda comes from the *giradillo*, or bronze weather vane, on the top, representing 'faith'. A life-sized replica is inside the cathedral.

Inside the tower, a series of ramps – wide enough to let the Moors ascend on donkeys – leads to the top, 94m (308ft) above the city with 360° views. The Moors used to have an observatory up here as well as using the minaret for the call to prayer. The top of La Giralda is in fact newer than the base; in the 14th century an earthquake damaged four ornamental globes that used to be here, and in the 16th century a belfry was installed.

At the base of the tower, the **Patio de los Naranjos**, Orange Tree Patio, is the only other surviving part of the mosque, with irrigation channels that would have filled the fountain in which the faithful washed themselves five times a day.

The only other Moorish relic of note in Sevilla is the **Torre de Oro**, the Golden Tower, which stands on the bank of the Guadalquivir River. Built by the **Almohads** in the 13th century as a guard tower, the 12-sided structure was covered with shimmering gold tiles. Later, it served as a prison and today houses a small naval museum.

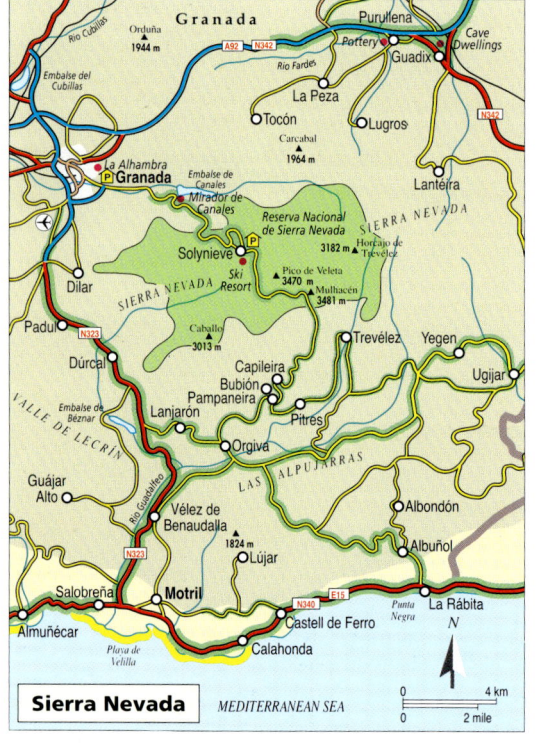

Sierra Nevada   *MEDITERRANEAN SEA*

The Cathedral ★★★

Sevilla's awe-inspiring cathedral is technically the largest in the world, just beating St Peter's in Rome and St Paul's in London in terms of volume, a fact of which the Sevillanos are extremely proud. When the Christians reconquered Sevilla in 1248, the Almohad mosque was used as a makeshift cathedral. In 1402, however, **King Pedro the Cruel** ordered a cathedral to be built, a project which took 104 years to complete. The sheer size inside, 42m (138ft) high, is breathtaking and the 43 chapels are richly decorated but the

most impressive structure of all is the **high altar**. Created by a single craftsman, **Pierre Dancart**, who spent most of his working life on this, the altar is the largest in the world, 27m (89ft) tall, and dazzling with gold-leaf covering 44 scenes from the New Testament. The top figures are larger to put the images in perspective, and some of them are over 2m (6½ft) tall.

The supposed remains of **Christopher Columbus** are situated by the entrance to the sacristy. His casket is held aloft by four figures representing the then four kingdoms of Spain: León, Castilla (Castile), Aragón and Navarra. León is holding an oar instead of a spear in honour of the sea voyages of the great explorer. Castilla's spear, meanwhile, is piercing a pomegranate, the Spanish for which is *granada*. It was in 1492, the year Columbus discovered the New World, that **Granada**, the last Moorish kingdom of Andalucía fell to the Christians, hence the symbolism.

Above: *La Giralda's minaret which was used to call the Moors to prayer.*

CARMEN'S TOBACCO FACTORY

Around 1750, it was unusual for women to work, especially in **Sevilla's** tobacco factory. Carmen and her friends would roll their own cigarettes from tobacco scraps, which gave them a rather unjust reputation as fast women. Above the door of the factory is a stone statue of an angel with a trumpet; the local saying was that the day a virgin crossed the threshold, the trumpet would sound. Not surprisingly, it never has.

Indian Archives *

Sevilla's former stock exchange, next to the cathedral,
houses the Indian Archives: maps and documentation
about the discovery of the **New World**. Only a small selection is on view but the archives provide an introduction to
the voyages which set sail from Sevilla. Open Monday–
Friday 10:00–14:00, closed weekends and holidays.

The Alcázar ***

Opposite the cathedral on the other side of the Plaza del
Triunfo, the Alcázar is one of the best surviving examples
of **Mudéjar** architecture, the part-Arab, part-Gothic and
part-Renaissance style adopted by Moors who worked
under the Christians. Most of the building today is the
work of King Pedro the Cruel who reigned in the 15th
century, although subsequent inhabitants have left their

mark. **Isabella I** added a
wing in 1503, from where
the negotiations for
Columbus' voyages were
carried out and **Charles V**
added a series of state
apartments later in the 16th
century. Most of the palace
is open to the public.

   The **Mudéjar** style has
adorned the palace with
exquisite mosaics and
stunning paintwork, par-
ticularly in the red, gold
and green half-dome ceil-
ing in the opulent **Salón
de los Embajadores**,
where Queen Isabella
received Columbus. Lions,
castles and animal figures,
however, give the style
away; Moors would never
have used such symbolism
in their own designs.

In the Chapel, **Alejo Fernandez'** painting of the **Virgen de los Mariantes** shows the Virgin of the Navigators watching over Columbus and his first crewmen. Charles V stands behind the virgin and the first conquered American Indians kneel in the background. Also fascinating is the **Patio de las Muñecas**, or Patio of the Dolls, so-called because of tiny doll faces carved on some of the arches. This was the **harem** in the original palace and the shuttered windows, *celosias* or *jalousies*, take their name from this era, when the women could see out but no-one could see in.

The gardens of the Alcázar, a mass of exotic perfumes in spring, are filled with flowering plants from the West Indies and South America, symbolic of specimens brought back by Columbus. The small pavilion overlooking the maze was built by Charles V.

Above: *Sevilla's Alcázar is a classic example of Mudejar architecture.*

Barrio Santa Cruz **

East of the cathedral is the Barrio Santa Cruz, formerly the Jewish quarter until its residents were expelled in 1492. Today, the shady, narrow streets are full of *tapas* bars and restaurants and open doors reveal tantalizing glimpses of surprisingly large patios, shaded by greenery and cooled by a central fountain. Gardens were and are very important to Sevillanos as the surrounding countryside is so barren. There's a permanent art exhibition in the **Hospicio de los Venerables Sacerdotes**, a former hospice, which is worth a visit.

Parque de María Luisa **

At weekends, this lush sub-tropical garden in the southeast of the city is where Sevillanos come to stroll past ornamental fountains and exotic floral displays. The park was the site of the 1929 Expo of the Americas and around its perimeter are magnificent pavilions in assorted

---

OPERA IN SEVILLA

Sevilla's romantic image inspired writers and composers throughout Europe and all of the following operas were set in the city:
- **Carmen** (Bizet)
- **The Barber of Seville** (Rossini)
- **The Marriage of Figaro** (Mozart)
- **Don Juan** (Mozart and various other composers; there are no less then 11 versions)
- **Fidelio** (Beethoven and various other composers)
- **La Fuerza del Destino** (Verdi)
- **La Favorita** (Prokofiev)
- **Conchita** (Zandonai)
- **Bodas en el Monasterio** (Prokofiev)

architectural styles representing the nations of the Americas. The Colombian building is now a consulate, and the Brazilian one is a police station. A Mudéjar pavilion now houses a folk museum and one of the mansions an archaeological museum. The highlight, however, is the sweeping expanse of the **Plaza de España**, a lavish building adorned with thousands of blue and white tiles. The semicircular design represents Spain welcoming the world with open arms and the four bridges the kingdoms of León, Castilla, Aragón and Navarra. Each of the ceramic pictures around the base depicts a province of Spain, complete with a map.

Expo '92

Twentieth-century man has left his own mark on the city's architecture with a cluster of glassy pavilions gleaming in the sun on **La Isla de la Cartuja**, an island in the Gualdalquivir River housing an old monastery and a former pottery. Seven stark, futuristic bridges linking the island to the city have already become symbols of Sevilla and the former Expo site is now being developed as a theme park.

Right: *The April Fair in Sevilla is Andalucía's most spectacular festival.*
Opposite: *Hundreds of marble columns in the Mezquita were originally from the Roman and Visigothic churches.*

CORDOBA

Two hours north of Málaga on the highway, Córdoba basks in the hot sun of the plains on the banks of the River Gualdalquivir, upstream from Sevilla. Founded in 152BC by the **Romans**, Córdoba later became the capital of Moorish Spain, a city of incredible wealth, learning and culture. From the 11th century, it was also a thriving **Jewish** community.

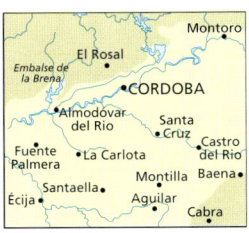

But like all Andalucían cities, Córdoba eventually fell to the **Christians**, succumbing in 1236, after which time its glory faded. Plagues, battering by the French in the Napoleonic wars and even more suffering during the **Spanish Civil War** further ran down the city. Now it exists as a pleasant regional centre, reasonably prosperous thanks to olive oil production and tourism.

La Mezquita ✴✴✴

Córdoba is essentially famous for one monument, La Mezquita, the most spectacular mosque ever built by the Moors and still beautifully preserved. Only the mosque at **Mecca** is larger. Open 10:00–19:30 Monday–Saturday; 14:00–19:00 Sundays and holidays.

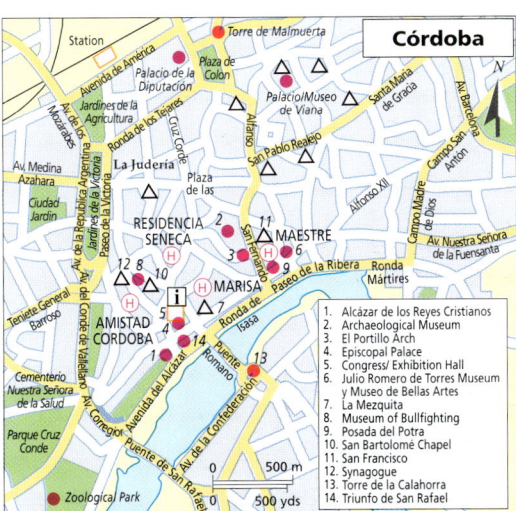

Córdoba

1. Alcázar de los Reyes Cristianos
2. Archaeological Museum
3. El Portillo Arch
4. Episcopal Palace
5. Congress/ Exhibition Hall
6. Julio Romero de Torres Museum y Museo de Bellas Artes
7. La Mezquita
8. Museum of Bullfighting
9. Posada del Potra
10. San Bartolomé Chapel
11. San Francisco
12. Synagogue
13. Torre de la Calahorra
14. Triunfo de San Rafael

Above: *Trees bearing bitter oranges grow all over Sevilla and Córdoba.*

The Mezquita was built by **Abd ar-Rahman I** on the site of a former **Visigothic** church, itself situated on top of a **Roman** temple. Started in 736, the original mosque was completed in 796. In the ninth century, **Córdoba** became a place of pilgrimage and by the 10th century, was one of the largest and most spectacular cities in Europe.

The entrance to the mosque is through the **Patio de los Naranjos**, a square lined with orange trees and the remnants of a fountain. Originally, there was no wall between the patio and the marble columns inside and the trees represented a continuation of the columns, filtering the strong sunlight to create a shady place in which to pray and contemplate. The columns, some 580 in total, come from Roman and Visigothic churches and are mostly marble, topped with red and white horseshoe-shaped arches.

The octagonal **Mihrab** chamber, pointing to Mecca, was added in the 10th century by al-Hakam II. Brilliantly coloured mosaics in gold, red and green, a gift from the Byzantine emperor Nicephoras Phocas II, adorn the walls, elaborate arches forming a dome overhead.

The cathedral, seemingly out of place, was added in 1523 by Charles V, who later regretted tampering with the mosque's simple beauty. The cathedral is worth visiting for its mahogany choir stalls, carved by **Pedro Duque Cornejo**. The **Capilla de Villaviciosa** nearby, built in 1377, is an elaborate example of Mudéjar architecture.

Around the Mezquita **

The narrow, whitewashed streets around the Mezquita are a riot of colour in summer, scarlet and pink geraniums cascading from every balcony. Northeast of the Mezquita, the **Callejón de los Flores** is one of the most beautiful.

Outside the mosque, the **Judería** is a fascinating tangle of narrow streets containing one of only three synagogues – this one built in 1315 – to survive the Christian reconquest of Andalucía. Nearby, there's a craft market and a bullfighting museum. West of the Mezquita is the **Alcázar**, a 14th-century Mudéjar palace on the riverbank. The shady gardens look out over the old Roman bridge over the Guadalquivir River and an original Moorish waterwheel.

PLAZA DEL POTRO

Named after its 16th-century fountain with a statue of a colt (*potro*), this atmospheric square close to the Mezquita is a national monument. Formerly a livestock market, the square and the restored 14th-century inn, the **Posada del Potro**, are mentioned by **Cervantes** in *Don Quixote*.

Also on the square is Córdoba's **Museum of Fine Arts**, housed in a 16th-century hospital. Across the courtyard is a small museum dedicated to the work of local artist **Julio Romero de Torres** (1885–1930).

THE SIERRA NEVADA

Spain's highest mountain range, the Sierra Nevada stretches from east to west between Granada and the Costa del Sol. Rugged and remote, the high peaks of **Veleta** (3470m; 11,385ft) and **Mulhacén** (3481m; 11,421ft) are covered in snow for much of the year, forming a spectacular backdrop to the city of Granada.

There are two routes into the mountains. The fast Veleta road from Granada is Europe's highest mountain road. From the south, a scenic but serpentine road climbs up through the Alpujarras, the magnificent foothills.

Skiing

On the exposed, north-facing slopes of Veleta is Europe's most southerly ski area, **Solynieve**. Pradollano, the village itself, is a purpose-built ski station and is not the world's most attractive, composed of modern buildings in a rather bleak setting. For a day's skiing in spring snow and hot sun, however, the resort is an added bonus for any skier visiting the Costa del Sol.

The resort is only 30 minutes from Granada or 1½ hours' drive from Málaga and is compact and easy to get around. Skiable terrain includes some 2500ha (6178 acres) of marked pistes in a wide open, treeless bowl with skiing up to 3000m (9843ft). Of the trails, 15 are graded easy, 16 intermediate and six difficult. Nineteen

ITALICA

The excavated city of Italica, close to **Sevilla**, is one of the best-preserved examples of Roman architecture in Spain. Attracted by the fertile plains of the Guadalquivir and the navigability of the river, the Romans grew and exported olives from this region on a massive scale and Italica, founded in 206BC by Scipio Africanus, became one of the major cities of the Roman Empire. Two emperors, **Trajan** and **Hadrian**, were born here and the city rose to military importance in the second and third centuries AD. A vast amphitheatre seating 25,000, theatre, baths, villas and houses with intact mosaics can all be visited and archaeologists are still digging, expecting to find more examples of grand buildings and lavish homes.

Left: *The high altitude of the Sierra Nevada makes it an ideal location for an observatory*

Above: Snow-capped peaks, steeply terraced slopes and white villages characterise the Alpujarras.

ski lifts whisk skiers up the mountain from the centre of the village.

Considerable sums were invested in improving the resort's facilities for the 1995 season, when the World Downhill Championships were supposed to be held here. A lack of snow meant the event was postponed until 1996 which spurred improvements for future skiers including new, faster lifts, night-time illumination of the El Río piste and a general facelift for the village. Everything the skier needs from equipment to ski tuition can be arranged in the resort.

The Veleta Summit

July and August are the only months when the highest mountain road in Spain is passable by car. This twisting dirt track heads over the summit of Veleta (3470m; 11,385ft) and keen hikers can walk the trail when the snow has cleared, starting from the *parador* outside the village. The trek is technically easy but nonetheless arduous – a good three hours to walk up and a further two hours down should be allowed. There are no facilities along the way but wildlife – goats and birds – is abundant and the views are breathtaking, with the Atlas Mountains of Morocco visible on a clear day.

All sorts of outdoor activities are arranged in the village in summer, including hang-gliding, mountain biking, horse-riding, archery and tennis. One of the most impressive sights in summer is brilliantly coloured paragliders descending from the mountain like a flock of exotic birds. Mountain bikers can try out some exciting terrain here; the Borreguiles gondola lift runs all summer, transporting bikes and riders to a network of marked trails, graded according to difficulty.

**SIERRA NEVADA
FLORA AND FAUNA**

The high peaks of the Sierra Nevada reveal over 2000 types of plant, several of which are native to this area. Above the snowline, spring is the best time to visit for the delicate *Narcissus nevadensis*, a rare **daffodil**, alongside **saxifrage** and **wormwood**, **buttercups** and **violets**.

Some 3000 **Spanish ibex** now inhabit this area and the greener, lower slopes support **wildcats** and **badgers**. Birds of prey breed on the high cliffs and on the lower slopes, **hoopoes**, **black redstarts**, **wheatears** and **rock thrushes** can be seen.

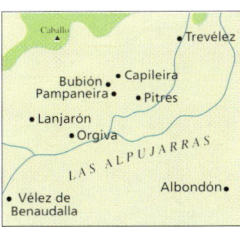

LAS ALPUJARRAS

The southern slopes of the Sierra Nevada, a series of valleys known as Las Alpujarras, are a revelation. Torrents gushing down from the snowy peaks of the Sierra have cut deep ravines in the soft rock and the lower slopes are brilliant green with crops growing in the fertile deposits. As the road climbs, olive groves give way to oak, pine and chestnut forests.

A distinctive feature of the area is the hill terraces, possibly started by the very early Ibero-Celtic settlers 2000 years ago. When the Moors lost Granada to the Catholic kings, they were allowed to settle in Las Alpujarras and for a while the area had a strong Muslim population. The Moors were eventually expelled in 1568 and Christian peasants from Galicia were moved here, which is how some villages and families come to have Galician names today.

In recent times, Las Alpujarras has languished in relative poverty, reviving only recently with the growth in ecotourism and an influx of foreign residents eager to escape city life in the cool mountain air. From the coast or from Granada, a comfortable day's drive takes in **Lanjarón**, **Orgiva**, **Pampaneira**, **Bubión** and **Capileira** before heading up to **Trevélez**, the highest village in Spain. The astonishingly clean air and stunning views make it tempting to stay longer and the area is full of hikers and mountain bikers.

JAMÓN SERRANO

The legs of ham hanging all over Trevélez are not local – the meat comes from pig farms downs on the plains – but the air gives the meat a special quality. First, it is buried in salt, one day for each kilo of ham, and then hung for a year or 18 months. Local restaurants serve the *jamón* as *tapas*, in slices with cheese, or cooked with fish and stews.

Villagers keep their own pigs for *jamón serrano*, but the animals eat a less selective diet than farmed pigs and tend to be more fatty.

Left: *Life moves at a slower pace in the high Alpujarras.*

Lanjarón and Orgiva *

Off the main Granada-Motril road, the first and most visited village is the spa of Lanjarón, one of the biggest **mineral water** producers in Spain. On the way up, beware of lorries thundering down the mountain road, laden with crates. Lanjarón's **spa baths** are thought to have curative powers and the village is busy in summer with elderly people coming in search of remedies for rheumatism and arthritis. Like most of the Alpujarras villages, Lanjarón has Moorish origins and there is a ruined castle below the main, tree-lined Avenida de Andalucía.

Orgiva, a busy little market town 11km (7 miles) further east, has good shopping in the colourful market. Things to look out for include woven rugs, baskets, local pottery and cured mountain ham. Orgiva is also the last petrol stop before heading into the high Alpujarras.

The High Alpujarras ***

The road now twists and turns in the foothills of **Mulhacén**, mainland Spain's highest mountain at 3481m (11,485ft), and soon reveals a deep gorge, **Poqueira**, with three tiny white villages perched high on the mountain terraces above: **Pampaneira**, **Bubión** and **Capileira**. The architecture is quite different here, built in the original style of mountain **Berber tribes** who lived here in Moorish times and only otherwise found in the Atlas Mountains of Morocco. Although many of the houses are whitewashed, some of the newer buildings are left as attractive coarse, grey slate in the original style, the walls extra thick as protection against the summer heat and winter storms. Another typical feature of the area is flat roofs, many of them crammed with flowers and window boxes.

Below: *Visitors can learn yoga and t'ai chi in the village of Bubión.*

All kinds of outdoor activities are arranged by specialist companies in these villages. Hiking in the mountains with a guide is very popular, following the old mule tracks that cross the Sierra from Granada to the coast.

Without a guide, a good map and a compass are essential and some of the walking is quite tough, although rewarding. Some people hike from village to village, staying in *posadas*, or tiny inns along the way. This can also be done on horseback or mountain bike. More extreme sports include parapenting (a form of hang gliding with a parachute), mountain climbing and four-wheel-drive expeditions off the road.

The area also attracts a new generation of New Age visitors – not hippies, but older, independent travellers in search of a spiritually fulfilling holiday. In **Bubión**, a company called Global Spirit arranges courses in yoga, meditation and t'ai chi, as well as painting, photography and pottery classes. Visits can be arranged to the Tibetan Buddhist Monastery of al-Atalaya, high on the mountain above the village, and birthplace of Osel, one of the first Buddhist lamas (priests) in the west.

A result of this 'green' tourist activity is that all three villages have enjoyed an influx of wealth. As well as being immaculately kept, tiny art galleries and restaurants serving a new kind of cuisine are flourishing, specializing in dishes that are Spanish but with very fresh ingredients and a strong emphasis on vegetables.

Trevélez **

A further 14km (9 miles) up the mountain road is Trevélez, built on three levels on the lip of a grassy ravine through which the **Rio Trevélez** flows. The scenery is bleaker up here with fewer trees and a cooler climate, covering the village with snow in winter and early spring. The exceptional quality of the mountain air makes this a famous spot for *jamón serrano* – cured ham.

Mountain trout is also fished in the river and every other whitewashed building advertises cured ham, trout and woven rugs. The local specialities, particularly river trout with slices of ham, are delicious. Some of the houses where the ham is hung can be visited. Several of the most testing hikes into the high peaks start here, although there are easier walks lower down the valley, fragrant with wild flowers and herbs.

Above: *Red chilli peppers hanging out to dry in the mountain air.*

Beyond the Coast at a Glance

BEST TIMES TO VISIT

Sevilla is at its best in **spring**, although hotels are full around the time of Holy Week and the April Fair, both of which fall around **Easter**. In summer, the city is too hot to explore on foot, reaching 40°C (104°F) on occasion. Córdoba has a similar climate. The Sierra Nevada is covered by snow in **winter** and is only worth visiting from **January** to **March** for skiers, as the high passes are blocked by snow. **July** and **August** are the best months for hiking, when it is possible to climb Veleta and Mulhacén, the highest peaks. The Alpujarras are lovely from late **spring** to **November**, when the first snows fall, although temperatures plummet at night outside the summer months.

GETTING THERE

Sevilla has an **international airport** and is served by **motorways** connecting the rest of Spain. **Coach** operators link the city with the Costa del Sol. A fast train, the **AVE**, makes the journey from Madrid in 2½ hours. From Madrid, the **AVE** train takes two hours. The Sierra Nevada and Las Alpujarras can be reached by road either from Granada or from the coast. **Domestic flights** serve Granada and there are regular **trains** from Madrid and Barcelona, with onward connections by bus.

GETTING AROUND

The centre of Sevilla is compact and easy to explore on foot, although **horse-drawn carriages** wait outside the cathedral for a more relaxing tour. Córdoba is the same; on a short visit, most sights are within walking distance. Otherwise, **taxis** are plentiful. Make sure the taxi driver uses the meter. Exploring the Sierra Nevada and the Alpujarras is easiest by **car**, as local **bus services** are slow, stopping in every village.

WHERE TO STAY

Sevilla
LUXURY
Hotel Alfonso XIII, San Fernando 2, 41004 Sevilla, tel: (95) 422-2862, fax: (95) 421-6033. Palatial, five-star, Gran Luxe where royals stay.
Hotel Tryp Colón, c/Canelejas 1, 41001 Sevilla, tel: (95) 422-2900, fax: (95) 422-0938. Mock-Regency hotel used by bullfighters.
Hotel Doña María, c/Don Remondo 19, 41004 Sevilla, tel: (95) 422-4990, fax: (95) 421-9546. Charming hotel close to cathedral.
Hotel Alcora, Ctra. San Juan-Tomares, 41920 San Juan Aznalfarache, tel: (95) 476-9400, fax: (95) 417-0128. Modern four-star hotel just outside centre.

MID-RANGE
Casas de la Judería, Callejon de Dos Fermanas 7, Plaza Santa María la Blanca, 41004 Sevilla, tel: (95) 441-5150, fax: (95) 422-2170. Collection of beautiful old houses in Jewish quarter converted into elegant, serviced apartments.

BUDGET
Hostal Plaza-Sevilla, c/Canelejas 2, 41001 Sevilla, tel: (95) 421-7149, fax: (95) 421-0773. Excellent hostel, designed by the same architect as the Plaza España.
Hotel Simon, c/Garcia Vinuesa 19, 41001 Sevilla, tel: (95) 422-6660, fax: (95) 456-2241. Small hotel in three old town houses.

Córdoba
LUXURY
Parador de Córdoba, Avenida de Arruzafa, 14012 Córdoba, tel: (957) 275-900, fax: (957) 200-409. Modern *parador* in quiet grounds.

MID-RANGE
Hotel Marisa, c/Cardenal Herrero 6, 14003 Córdoba, tel: (957) 473-142. Simple, rooms opposite La Mezquita.

BUDGET
Hostal Maestre, c/Romero Barros 4, 14003 Córdoba, tel: (957) 472-410. Charming hostel off the Plaza del Potro.

Sierra Nevada
All the hotels in **Pradollano** tend to be modern and rather bleak, characteristic of a purpose-built ski village.

Beyond the Coast at a Glance

LUXURY

Hotel Melia Sierra Nevada, Pradollano S/N, 18196 Sierra Nevada, tel: (958) 480-400, fax: (958) 480-458. Modern hotel, part of Melia chain, in centre of ski resort.

MID-RANGE

Parador Nacional Sierra Nevada, Ctra. Sierra Nevada km35, 18196 Sierra Nevada, tel: (958) 480-200, fax: (958) 480-212. *Parador* located above Pradollano village overlooking the ski slopes.

BUDGET

Hotel Telecabina, Plaza de Pradollano, 18196 Sierra Nevada, tel: (958) 289-120, fax: (958) 249-140. One-star ski lodge in the resort centre next to lift station.

Las Alpujarras

There is plenty of accommodation in Capileira, Bubión, Orgiva and Lanjarón and companies like **Nevadensis** will book rooms.

MID-RANGE

Villa Turistica del Poqueira, 18412 Bubión (Granada), tel: (958) 763-111, fax: (958) 763-136. Comfortable, low-rise hotel run by local cooperative.

BUDGET

Mesón Poqiera, c/Doctor Castilla 6, 18413 Capiliera (Granada), tel: (958) 763-048. This is a basic hostel, but it has an excellent restaurant.

WHERE TO EAT

Sevilla

La Albahaca, Plaza de Santa Cruz 12, tel: (95) 456-1204. Andalucian décor, good fish and game. Closed Sundays.
Meson Don Raimundo, c/Argote de Molina 26, tel: (95) 422-3355. Andalucian food. Closed Sunday dinner.
Tapas: **The Triana district**, just across the river from the cathedral, is lined with *tapas* bars, frequented by locals. As a guide for good food, always go where the locals go.

Córdoba

El Caballo Rojo, Cardenal Herrero 28, Córdoba, tel: (957) 475-375. Andalucian dishes with an Arab influence – try lamb in honey and monkfish with pine nuts.
Bar Sociedad de Plateros, San Francisco 6, Córdoba. Lively bar near centre with wide choice of food and great *tapas*. Good value for money.

Las Alpujarras

Meson La Fragua, c/San Antonio 4, Trevélez, tel: (958) 858-573. Popular with hikers, Alpujarrian food. Closed from 10 January to 10 February.

Bar Frenfría, Ctra. de la Sierra, 18412 Bubión, Granada, tel: (958) 763-234. Located next to a mountain stream. The views are great and regional specialities are served here.

TOURS AND EXCURSIONS

All the travel agents who have their offices along the Costa del Sol will book excursions to Sevilla and Córdoba – each a day trip and a long coach ride. It's worth staying overnight in both towns to enjoy the atmosphere.
Guidetur, an association of independent, knowledgable guides in Sevilla, will conduct private sightseeing tours. Contact them at tel: (95) 422-2374, fax: (95) 456-1245.
Nevadensis, tel: (958) 763-127, runs guided walks and pony-trekking as well as mountain activities.

USEFUL CONTACTS

Tourist Information, Sevilla, tel: (95) 422-1404.
Tourist Information, c/Torrijos 10, Córdoba, tel: (957) 471-235.
Pradollano Hotels, reservations, tel: (958) 249-243.

SEVILLA	J	F	M	A	M	J	J	A	S	O	N	D
AVERAGE TEMP. °C	11	12	14	17	20	25	28	28	24	20	15	12
AVERAGE TEMP. °F	52	54	57	63	68	77	82	82	75	69	59	54
HOURS OF SUN DAILY	5	6	7	8	10	11	11	11	10	8	5	5
RAINFALL mm	100	100	100	75	50	13	-	-	25	50	50	75
RAINFALL in	4	4	4	3	2	0.5	-	-	1	2	2	3
DAYS OF RAINFALL	8	7	7	7	1	1	-	-	2	6	6	7

Travel Tips

Tourist Information

The Spanish Tourist Board has offices in the **United Kingdom** (London); the **USA** (Chicago, Los Angeles, Miami and New York); **Canada** (Toronto); **Australia** (Sydney) and most **European** countries. The **Costa del Sol** also has its own **Promotion Board: Patronato Provincial de Turismo**, Calle Compositor Lehmberg Ruiz, 3, 29007 Málaga, tel: (95) 228-8354, fax: (95) 228-6042. There are local tourist information offices in most towns and resorts, including **Benalmádena Costa**, **Ronda**, **Torremolinos**, **Antequera**, **Estepona**, **Fuengirola**, **Marbella**, **Nerja**, **Jerez**, **Granada**, **Sevilla**, **Córdoba** and **Almería**.

Entry Requirements

All visitors need a passport or in certain cases, an identity card. Citizens of **Andorra**, **Liechtenstein**, **Monaco**, **Switzerland** and countries within the **EU** need only present an identity card with the exception of **Denmark** and the **UK**, citizens of which need a passport. UK visitors must have a full 10-year passport as of 1995. **US**, **Canadian** and **Japanese** citizens require a passport but no visa. Visas are required by citizens of **Australia** and **New Zealand**. All visitors can stay for a period of up to 90 days, after which time a residence permit is required. **UK** citizens can stay up to six months before a residence permit is required.

Customs

The maximum allowance for duty-free items brought into Spain is as follows: one litre of spirits or two of fortified wine; two litres of wine and 200 cigarettes. When bought and duty paid in the EU, the amounts are 10 litres of spirits, 90 litres of wine and 110 litres of beer, for private consumption only. Duty-free sales within the EU were abolished in June 1999.

Spanish and foreign currency, banker's drafts and traveller's cheques can be imported and exported without being declared up to a limit of 1,000,000 pesetas. Spanish customs are generally polite and easy to negotiate but travellers coming in from Morocco are subject to stringent searches.

Health Requirements

No vaccinations are required to enter Spain and the only real health hazards are the occasional upset stomach and the sun, which is very strong during the **summer** months of **June** to **September**. Visitors travelling onwards to **Morocco** should have polio and typhoid boosters to be on the safe side but it is essential to check the exact require-ments with the Moroccan embassy beforehand.

EU citizens qualify for free medical treatment on presen-tation of the appropriate form (the E111 for British citizens). Visitors from elsewhere should arrange their own travel and medical insurance.

Getting There

The Costa del Sol can be reached by air, rail, road and boat. **Málaga** is the principal port and airport. **By Air:** Málaga and Sevilla both have modern airports served direct by **Iberia**, the national airline of Spain, from most European cities. Málaga, however, is the main gateway to the **Costa del Sol** and in summer gets very busy with charter flights. **Gibraltar** is a more convenient gateway from **London** to the western side of the Costa del Sol, served by regular flights with **GB Airways**, a subsidiary of British Airways. Passengers travelling through Gibraltar should note that its entry requirements are the same as for Great Britain. **Granada** also has a domestic airport with flights to **Madrid** and other Spanish cities and **Jerez** is served by **GB Airways** from the UK. No airport tax on departure.

Iberia Airlines of Spain: for flight information as well as reservations: tel: (95) 213-6166.

GB Airways: tel: (350) 79-200.

By Rail: Rail travel can be confusing in Spain as there are several different types of service. A new high-speed train, **AVE**, links Madrid with Córdoba in two hours, with a connection onwards to Málaga in four hours. Long-distance trains, **RENFE**, take eight hours from Madrid to Málaga and there are direct daily trains to Málaga and Granada from Barcelona. Local trains are called **Talgo** and link Málaga with regional towns of Andalucía through-out the day.

The **Moto/Auto Express** service carries cars and motor-bikes on the train and there

are various saver passes for visitors using the railway net-work but check these before leaving home as some of the best deals are only available outside Spain.

By Car: Travellers bringing their own car and residing outside the EU must have a **Green Card**, as third party insurance is compulsory. An international driving licence is required. Driving in Spain is on the right.

Car Hire: There are several car hire companies based at Málaga Airport and most have offices in the main resorts. Drivers must be over 21 with at least one year's experience. Never leave anything in a car as vehicle crime is a problem. Cars can be hired in Gibraltar and taken to Spain, but must be returned to Gibraltar.

ROAD SIGNS

Aduana ● customs
Autopista (de peaje) ●
Motorway/highway (toll)
Ceda el paso ● Give way
Circunvalación ● ring road
or bypass
Cruce peligroso ●
dangerous crossroads
Despacio ● slow
Desviación ● diversion
Entrada ● entrance
Obras ● workmen
Prohibido adelantar ●
no overtaking
Estacionamento prohibido ●
no parking
Sin plomo ● unleaded petrol
Salida ● exit
Salida de camiones ●
lorry exit
Puesto de soccoro ●
first aid post

Spanish rental cars may not be taken into Gibraltar; park at La Línea and walk across instead. **Avis**, Cortina del Muelle, Málaga, tel: (95) 221-6627. **Hertz**, Alameda de Colón 17, Málaga, tel: (95) 222-5597. **Autos Lara**, Calle Salvador Allende S/N, Torremolinos, tel: (95) 138-1800.

Road conditions and travel information are available in Spanish on the **Teleruta service**, tel:(91) 535-2222.

Petrol: Petrol stations are widely available with leaded and lead-free petrol and diesel. Some are self-service and some have attendants.

By Boat: Ferries sail to **Melilla** and **Ceuta**, two Spanish dependencies in North Africa, from Málaga and Algeciras respectively. There are also ferry and hydrofoil services from Algeciras and Benalmádena to **Tangier**. Cruise lines call at Málaga, Algeciras and occasionally, Motril. **Transmediterranea**, c/Juan Diaz 4, Málaga, tel: (95) 222-4391.

What to Pack

Dress on the Costa del Sol is **informal** with many visitors spending most of their time in beachwear. Respect, how-ever, should be shown when entering cathedrals and churches and when exploring out of the way villages, which tend to be inhabited by old people. Some of the smarter hotels in Marbella have a dress code of jacket and tie and younger people usually dress up in the evenings to

visit the many nightclubs.
Golf clubs also require the
usual golfer's dress code.
Walking boots are advisable
for hiking in Las Alpujarras
and the Serranía de Ronda
and visitors should remember
that the climate can be a lot
cooler at altitude. Shops and
department stores stock all
major items.

Money Matters

Currency: The unit of currency
is the **peseta**, which comes in
coins of 1, 5, 10, 25, 50, 100,
200 and 500 and notes of
1000, 2000, 5000 and 10,000.
New coins are being phased in
but old ones are still accepted.
Banks: Banking hours are
09:00–14:00 Monday–Friday
and 09:00–13:00 on

Saturdays, although they
vary occasionally from
branch to branch.
Credit Cards: All major credit
cards are accepted although
some country restaurants in
villages and small *tapas* bars
may require cash.
Holders of cards bearing the
Visa, **Mastercard**, **Cirrus** and
Plus signs can use Spanish
automatic tellers, which have
instructions in English.
Currency Exchange: Foreign
currency and travellers'
cheques can be changed in
banks and the **Bureaux de
Change** which operate in
the main resorts.
Taxes: Spanish sales tax (**IVA**)
is currently 16% and is not
always included in the price.
**Tipping and Service
Charges:** Tipping is optional;
around 10% of the price of
a meal is acceptable. Petrol
pump attendants and taxi
drivers also expect a small tip.

Accommodation

Hotels are rated with a star
system with five stars being
the highest. '*Gran Luxe*'
signifies a particularly luxurious hotel. Apartment hotels
follow the same grades, the
only difference being that
they have cooking facilities in
the rooms. *Hostals* and *pen-
siones*, which are more basic
establishments, are graded
from one to three stars.
Camp sites are rated luxury,
first, second and third class
and are plentiful. Each
region, however, is responsible for its own classification,
so accommodation gradings
will vary. Most villages have

rooms for hire – look out
for signs saying '*se alquilar*'.
Anybody wanting to stay in
a protected area, either
camping or in a mountain
refuge, should contact the
**environmental protection
agency: RAAR**, Apdo 2035,
04080 Almería tel: (951) 265-
018, fax: (951) 264-240.
Paradors are state-run
hotels, usually in historical
buildings or areas of out-
standing natural beauty.
Contact **Paradores de
Turismo**, c/Requena 8,
28013 Madrid, tel: (91) 516-
6666, fax. (91) 516-6657.
Estancias de España, a
private association of hotels
and restaurants in historic
buildings, produces a
brochure detailing its 44
members, 15 of which are
in Andalucía. **Estancias de
España**, c/Menendez Pidal,
31, bajo izqd, – local 28036
Madrid, tel: (91) 345-4141,
fax: (91) 345-5174.

Eating out

The **Costa del Sol** has various different types of eating
establishment. *Tapas* bars,
tascas, *bodegas*, *cervece-
rias* and *tabernas* are all
types of bar serving food.
A *comedor* is a simple dining
room, usually attached to a
bar and a *venta* is a similar
setup in the countryside,
usually with a small shop as
well. Restaurants are graded
one to five forks, but this
relates to price rather than
quality. A *marisqueria*
restaurant specializes in
seafood and an *asado*
in barbecued food.

Transport

Air: Domestic flights are operated by **Iberia**, its subsidiary **Viva Air** and **Aviaco**, with an efficient network linking Spain's major cities. Domestic flights operate from Málaga, Granada, Sevilla and Jerez.

Road: Southern Spain has an efficient dual carriageway network, much improved since the Expo in Sevilla in 1992. Some *autopistas* in Spain are toll roads but the only section in Andalucía to carry a charge is between Sevilla and Jerez.

Málaga and Sevilla both have ring roads and signposting everywhere is good, even on the mountain roads. Speed limits are 120kph (75mph) on autopistas, 120, 100 or 80kph (75, 62, 50mph) according to signs on *autovias* (dual carriageways), 90kph (56mph) on country roads and 60kph (37mph) on urban roads. Stiff, on the spot speeding fines are not uncommon. Wearing of seatbelts is compulsory in the front and if fitted, in the back. Motorcyclists must wear safety helmets by law.

Rail: *see* 'Rail Travel'.

Bus: Private bus companies provide regular links between major towns and all the outlying villages. **Alsina Graells Sur**, tel: (95) 284-1365, links Málaga with Córdoba and Granada and covers the routes from Málaga to the eastern Costa del Sol – Vélez-Málaga, Nerja and Motril. Along the western Costa del Sol, **Automóviles Portillo** links Málaga with Fuengirola, Marbella, Estepona and Algeciras, stopping at the villages in between, and serves Ronda and Coín, tel: (95) 287-2262. Timetables and fares are available from all the tourist offices and bus stations.

Business Hours

Shops and businesses generally open from 09:00–10:00 to 13:30–14:00, then close for a *siesta* and reopen from 16:00–20:00.

Some businesses start much earlier; around 08:00 and work straight through to 15:00 with no *siesta*. Hours also change in the summer. Big department stores now stay open all day but most supermarkets close for lunch.

<table>
<tr><td colspan="3">CONVERSION CHART</td></tr>
<tr><td>FROM</td><td>TO</td><td>MULTIPLY BY</td></tr>
<tr><td>Millimetres</td><td>Inches</td><td>0.0394</td></tr>
<tr><td>Metres</td><td>Yards</td><td>1.0936</td></tr>
<tr><td>Metres</td><td>Feet</td><td>3.281</td></tr>
<tr><td>Kilometres</td><td>Miles</td><td>0.6214</td></tr>
<tr><td>Kilometres square</td><td>Square miles</td><td>0.386</td></tr>
<tr><td>Hectares</td><td>Acres</td><td>2.471</td></tr>
<tr><td>Litres</td><td>Pints</td><td>1.760</td></tr>
<tr><td>Kilograms</td><td>Pounds</td><td>2.205</td></tr>
<tr><td>Tonnes</td><td>Tons</td><td>0.984</td></tr>
<tr><td colspan="3">To convert Celsius to Fahrenheit: x 9 ÷ 5 + 32</td></tr>
</table>

NATIONAL HOLIDAYS

January 1 •
New Year's Day
January 6 •
Epiphany
March or April •
Good Friday
May 1 •
May Day
August 15 •
Assumption
October 12 •
National Day
November 1 •
All Saints
December 6 •
Constitution Day
December 8 •
Immaculate Conception
December 25 •
Christmas Day

Lunch tends to be served from about 13:00–16:00, with dinner from 20:00 (sometimes earlier for the benefit of tourists) to 23:00. Bars and clubs stay open late on the coast – sometimes until 04:00.

Time Difference

Spain is one hour ahead of GMT in winter. From the last Sunday in March to the last Sunday in October it is two hours ahead.

Communications

The international dialling code for Spain is +34. Each province has its own dialling prefix – Málaga, for example, is (95), Cádiz (956). When dialling from within the province, include the prefix. The international code for Gibraltar is +350. Dialling from Spain, the prefix is (9567). Cheap rates are between 22:00 and 08:00.

GOOD READING

- Alastair Boyd, *The Sierras of the South*, (Flamingo, 1994). Englishman's love affair with southern Spain.
- Gerald Brenan, *The Face of Spain*, (Penguin, 1987). Essays on travels through Spain during Franco's dictatorship.
- *South From Granada*, (Penguin). Traveller's classic about life in the Alpujarras in the 1920s.
- Jan Morris, *Spain*, (Penguin, 1982). Account of life in Spain in the 1960s.
- Laurie Lee, *As I Walked Out One Midsummer Morning*, (Penguin); *A Rose for Winter*, (Penguin), *A Moment of War*, (Penguin). Lee's walk through Spain to Málaga; his time in Andalucia 20 years later; and an account of fighting in the Spanish Civil War.
- Ernest Hemingway, *Fiesta* or *The Sun Also Rises*, (Random House). Love story set in Andalucia during the civil war. *Death in the Afternoon*, (Random House). Detailed prose about bullfighting, written when Hemingway was in Ronda.
- Washington Irving, *Tales of the Alhambra*, (first published 1832, now available in bookshops all over Granada). Fact and fiction about life and love in the Alhambra.
- Federico García Lorca, *Five Plays: Comedies and Tragicomedies*, (Penguin) and *Selected Poems*. Plays and poems from Andalucia's most famous author.
- Ernest García and Andrew Paterson, *Where to Watch Birds in Southern Spain*, (HELM). Useful and practical guide to bird-watching in Andalucia, complete with maps and migration details.

Public telephones take coins of 5, 25 and 100 **pesetas**. To call overseas, dial 007 and wait for the tone to change before dialling the country code and the number. Telephone cards and stamps can be bought from **Telefónica** offices or **tobacconists**.
Post Offices: are open Monday–Saturday, 09:00–14:00.

Electricity

The power system is 220 or 225 volts AC. Older buildings occasionally have 110 or 125 volts AC and should be treated with extreme caution. Two-pin plugs are used. Americans will need a transformer, British visitors an adaptor.

Weights andMeasures

Spain uses the metric system.

Health Precautions

An excess of **sun** and *sangria* are the worst health problems encountered by most people. Use a high factor sun protection cream, wear a hat and take special care during the height of summer. Tap water is safe to drink in Spain, although mineral water is available everywhere. Mosquito repellant is recommended. Spanish pharmacists can dispense medicines often only available on prescription elsewhere. Opening hours are 09:00–13:30; 17:00–20:30 (with the occasional half-hour variation). Every area has a duty pharmacy with a 24-hour service, the address of which is displayed on the doors of other pharmacies.

Personal Safety

Petty crime is the only likely problem travellers might encounter, although the big cities have their no-go areas at night. Follow normal precautions: don't leave anything in a car; be careful with purses and wallets; don't wear ostentatious jewellery and use hotel safe deposit boxes. Remember that some inland areas are very poor, so bag snatching is more of a temptation. Sexual harassment is not generally a big problem and as the streets are always so busy at night, women travellers should feel safe walking around resorts.

Emergencies

Emergency numbers vary from town to town, although the **Policía Nacional** has one number **(091)** nationwide. Dial **(092)** for the **Policía Municipal**, or in Málaga, tel: (95) 221-2415. Other emergency numbers for Málaga are:
Fire brigade, tel: 080.
Medical emergencies, tel: 061.

Etiquette

Topless sunbathing is acceptable on beaches but more modesty is appropriate inland around lakes and in national parks. There are two nudist beaches (*playa nudista*) on the Costa del Sol, at Estepona and outside Fuengirola.

INDEX